Creating a Soap & Skin Care Brand

IT'S NOT ENOUGH TO MAKE GREAT PRODUCTS

by

Benjamin D. Aaron

Creating a Soap & Skin Care Brand

Copyright © 2017 by Benjamin D. Aaron

All rights reserved. No part of this publication may be reproduced, distributed, or transmitted in any form or by any means, including photocopying, recording, or other electronic or mechanical methods, without the prior written permission of the publisher, except in the case of brief quotations embodied in critical reviews and certain other noncommercial uses permitted by copyright law. For permission requests, write to the publisher at the email address below.

bda7b9@gmail.com

Printed in the United States of America

First Printing, 2017

Ordering Information: Wholesale sales. Special discounts are available on quantity purchases. For details, contact the publisher at the email address above.

ISBN-13: 978-1979412896

ISBN-10: 1979412898

Creating a Soap & Skin Care Brand

DEDICATION

This book is dedicated to all the brave men and women in the handcrafted soap and skin care industry who have made the choice to be successful.

Creating a Soap & Skin Care Brand

Creating a Soap & Skin Care Brand

CONTENTS

Introduction	Page 9
Chapter 1: Quick Checklist	Page 13
Chapter 2: Money Mentality	Page 19
Chapter 3: Success is a Decision	Page 37
Chapter 4: Mission, Vision & Values	Page 65
Chapter 5: Style Matters	Page 75
Chapter 6: What's in a Name?	Page 105
Chapter 7: Your Customer	Page 133
Chapter 8: Product Variation & Revenue Streams	Page 153
Chapter 9: Scalability, Hiring & Salary	Page 185
Chapter 10: Creating Hype	Page 209
Conclusion	Page 231
About the Author	Page 237
Suggested Reading	Page 239

Creating a Soap & Skin Care Brand

Creating a Soap & Skin Care Brand

ACKNOWLEDGEMENTS

A very special thank you to my beautiful wife, Amanda. I wouldn't be the person I am without you.

Creating a Soap & Skin Care Brand

INTRODUCTION

Though not blatantly obvious in the writing, this book is really about new beginnings. Having an established business doesn't mean you have to stick to what you already know if you feel an urge inside you to change. The only constant you really have is change, and the willingness to accept it as you move forward will ultimately define your success in this burgeoning, cottage industry. You can't learn from what you already know. The most successful entrepreneurs are experts in one simple thing above all else, and that is learning. Entrepreneurs are experts at learning new concepts, new methods and new advances to the betterment of not only their company, but themselves. My ultimate aim in writing this book is for you to learn a thing or two and encourage you to take massive action towards implementing any and all newfound knowledge you find here.

Furthermore, whether you are just starting out or have been in the game for a few years, this book is also about opening your eyes to the profound, progressive consequences of developing a true brand and not just a hobbyist's weekend plaything. And don't get me wrong. There is nothing criminal with being a hobbyist soapmaker who makes a few bucks here and there. If that is your shtick, more power to you. But I wrote this book specifically for folks who want to earn their keep from their business.

The ideas in this book were developed over my time spent as a start-up business coach in the soapmaker industry. From my experience, I offer lessons learned, insights from clients and some socialized thought-patterns that we might all be better off avoiding.

This book is about thinking bigger and then acting on those bigger, emboldened thoughts. People have done some crazy, awesome things in this world and were paid handsomely for it. These crazy, awesome things—whether it be an amazing new line of skin care products or the development of the first smartphone—all started as an idea. Maybe they were walking the dog when they thought of it. Maybe they were drunk at a bar with friends. Maybe they dreamed it. Maybe it was an idea they've had since they were children. However it came to be, they took their crazy, awesome idea and made it into a *thing*. They conceptualized it into our world. From a mere thought, they ultimately created a living for themselves that most people can't dream of. You can do that, too. By thinking outside the box, you can ultimately create an incredibly lucrative and nourishing life.

And this crazy, awesome idea of yours is the foundation you can build upon to further a strong set of values for yourself and your company. Your business can be incredibly unique if you allow yourself the time to create, imagine, dream and write. Solitude is underrated. Allow yourself to be alone with a pen and paper. Dream up your wildest ideas and transfer them onto paper. Your creativity is absolutely matchless. Don't let it stay dormant. Take the rather simple concepts from this book and conjure up a brand that will ultimately earn you a living.

This book is not about manufacturing, pricing or even selling. If you want recipes, you've come to the wrong place. If you are reading this, I already know you are a good soapmaker. I already know you make good products. I'm not going to showcase in this book something you already know how to do well. This book is about creativity, fun and a willingness to think and feel your way into developing a brand that people will fall in love with, simply by taking the time to do it.

I would strongly advise you to read the entire book, even if you think you already have a handle on an aspect of your company that the book delves into, such as a company name, or a strong mission statement. You still might find some insight and perhaps even a new outlook on what you can do moving forward, such as establishing a new DBA (doing business as) under your current company so that you can start fresh with a new company name and concept and still keep your same EIN number. You never know what might come up as you read, though you might predispose yourself to the contrary before reading. Even if you have a company and have started the selling process, read the entirety of the book to garner some clues and insights that you might not have thought all the way through.

COME ORIGINAL

I love music. I love art. I love funky concepts and the liberation of normal. From a business origination standpoint, I appreciate innovation and creativity above all else. In a word, I welcome and respect ORIGINALITY more than anything.

One of my favorite songs from the band, "311" is *Come Original*. The lyrics offer a strong suggestion to the bands' peers—fellow entertainers—to come strong in their originality and uniqueness. They don't want to go to an event and see a colleague who isn't a true novelty:

> *You got to come original, you got to come original*
> *All entertainers come original*
> *You got to come original, you got to come original*
> *All entertainers*
> *Hear why*
> *To come original it ain't nothin' strange*
> *You got to represent you got come full range*
> *Full range of emotion full range of styles*
> *When you come to town you'll have them comin' for miles*
> *and come original, you got to come original*
> *All entertainers come original*
> *You got to come original, you got to come original*

I want you to come original. Think way outside the box. Get rid of the box. Burn it, and start fresh, stark naked.

Be you. Do you. Be wildly creative with your company. Do things your own way. Name your products in your own style and flair. Conjure up product descriptions that really wow people when they read them. Be a bit daring and bold in the messages your company gives.

Think outlandishly funky with your company, and you will be successful. Don't follow the status quo. Don't jump on someone else's wagon. The business gods do not reward copy and paste. Come original.

~ Benjamin

CHAPTER 1:

QUICK CHECKLIST

Logistically speaking, starting a business in the U.S. is an incredibly easy undertaking. Taking a simple, step-by-step approach to all the details of creating a name, obtaining an EIN, opening an account, etc. takes as little as a day or two. Below is a brief overview list of to-dos to start a soap and skin care business. Even if you've already got a business underway, give the following a quick once-over. If you don't yet have your own business, take a look at the steps below and then fine-tune your details with the help of the IRS (Internal Revenue Service) and the SBA (Small Business Administration). A very helpful site to get you going in the right direction can be found at https://www.irs.gov/businesses/small-businesses-self-employed/checklist-for-starting-a-business.

Before we get started, please know that I am not an attorney, nor am I an accountant. The tips below are guidelines to help you learn what is needed to start your soap business. Be sure to consult with an attorney or tax professional when it comes to questions about which business structure to form (discussed later in the book), how to handle your accounting and for help with tax liability.

DECIDE ON A BUSINESS NAME

What will you call your business? We have an entire chapter dedicated to the power of a company name, so keep reading if you don't already have one (read the chapter even if you do). Once you select a business name, immediately check to see if the website domain is available. If the domain is taken, then you'll probably need to pick another name (this subject matter will also be discussed later in the book). Perform some Internet searches to see if anybody is using the name in business. You don't want to choose a name that someone else is using.

Search through the USPTO trademark database, found at https://www.uspto.gov/trademark, to see if anyone has or is in the process of trademarking the name. Obtain the URL. You don't have to build your website right away, but you want to own the domain before someone else grabs it.

Set your company name up on all of the popular social media sites such as Facebook, Twitter, Instagram…etc. Again, you don't have to start using them right away, but you want to procure them so that someone else doesn't swoop in and take them.

CHOOSE YOUR BUSINESS STRUCTURE

Determining the legal structure of your business is important. You'll have a few options, which come with various tax and legal implications. Two structures that I recommend when starting out are either a Sole Proprietorship or a Limited Liability Company (LLC). There are also General Partnerships, Limited Liability Partnerships, S-Corporations and C-Corporations. Before setting up your business, conduct research at www.sba.gov or consult an expert, such as a lawyer or accountant, to help you decide on the right legal structure to fit your circumstances.

OBTAIN AN EIN

A federal employer identification number, or EIN, is a nine-digit number the IRS assigns to businesses for tax filing and reporting purposes. You will also need it if you plan to have employees. A bank might require an EIN to open up a business account for your new company. Obtain an EIN before you visit your bank.

OPEN A BANK ACCOUNT

You'll need a bank account to put business money in and pay expenses from. Do not mingle personal money and business money, as this can create an accounting nightmare. Open both a checking and savings account. A savings account is great for tucking away money set aside to pay taxes or scaling up your equipment down the road.

STATE LICENSES AND REGISTRATIONS

Check your state website to see if your state requires licenses (business license) or for you to register your business in any way (such as for state taxes).

COLLECTING PAYMENT

You'll need to decide how people and other companies will pay you. Will you accept cash, checks and credit/debit cards? Then you'll need to utilize the services of a merchant account, such as Square or PayPal. These merchant account services have become the norm for small businesses.

ACCOUNTING

As a business, you will need to track your income and expenses. You can do this by using a spreadsheet or you can use a software program, such as QuickBooks.

Because entire books are written on accounting (and I highly recommend that you read some), I'm not going to go into detail here. I recommend that you hire the help of an accountant or take accounting classes to get you started. Many cities offer small business classes at community centers and colleges.

Every dollar that you collect needs to be accounted for and every expense needs to be recorded, as expenses reduce your taxable income. Taxes will need to be paid based on your income, per your business structure. An accountant can help determine which tax documents need to be filed (there are usually both state and federal) and when.

I highly recommend getting accounting software to help you keep track of income and expenses. I personally use QuickBooks Online, but there are several to choose from:

→ QuickBooks, FreshBooks, Wave

COLLECT AND PAY SALES TAX

You will be responsible for collecting sales tax on your product sales. Check your state's website for the rate that you are supposed to collect and information on how to pay it. Most states have an online payment system to allow you to pay sales tax. If you aren't making much, your state might have you pay sales tax annually. If you make a certain amount (varies by state) then your state might have you pay quarterly (or more).

You'll need to pay taxes on any money earned through your business (assuming you make a profit). Don't get caught at tax time with no money for Uncle Sam. If you open a savings account, put money aside as you bring in income. Set a standard percentage and stick to it.

INSURANCE

If you want to sell your products, I highly recommend that you get insurance. Because we live in a litigious society, you want to make sure that you are protected in case your products damage something or injure someone. Besides, many craft fairs, farmer's markets and retail stores require insurance if you want to sell your products.

We will cover broad topics in this book that pertain to creating a true brand. I have a list of suggested reading at the end of the book that will cover in great detail the ins and outs of business start-up logistics, tax information, business structuring, insurance and the like. I highly encourage you to become an expert in almost all of these fields, as business owners need to have this knowledge at the ready.

CHAPTER 2:

MONEY MENTALITY

I used to have a very misguided, "saintly" attitude about money that truly got in the way of my authentic efforts toward a successful business. In fact, I used to hate money, and I know I wasn't the only one. Through my own life experiences and shifting attitudes, to books and books of research to coaching and consulting one-on-one, I have found that a lot of people in the world hate money. Their relationship with money stems from an upbringing of spiritual piety and an abhorrence of greed.

But, we must be very careful with how we view greed. Greed is in the eye of the beholder. Greed is very subjective. By my judging others as greedy and materialistic because they had more money than me was an immensely egotistical and self-centered way of thinking, and it perpetuated a mentality of lack and envy deep inside me. This mentality of lack and envy only brought about people, circumstances and events that urged me to feel *even more* lack and envy. It was a never-ending, self-fulfilling prophecy of financial scarcity.

The mentality you have about money will dictate your financial future, period. Your bank account is driven by your financial thoughts and feelings. If you want more money in your life, but don't prepare for it, more money will never come. Or, if you want more money in your life, yet you think it is greedy or bad, more money will never come. You can't have *both* thoughts and expect a financially fruitful outcome! Prepare for money and learn to love it as a tool, just like a carpenter loves his hammer.

TOM & DICK

Two gentlemen, Tom and Dick—the exact same age, height, weight, income level, living arrangements and physical attributes—are each lonely and wish to find a partner.

Tom, a pleasant man with a positive attitude, is excited about the opportunity to find a life-long partner to be with. Dick is not as positively motivated.

Tom's home is clean, as he is in constant anticipation of meeting someone at any moment. He makes sure to sleep on "his" side of the bed and not in the middle, so as to prepare for the love of his life sleeping next to him. The rack that holds his clothes in the closet is only half-full so that his soon-to-be partner will have adequate space for her clothes. Though he could use both drawers in his bathroom vanity for his things, he only uses one to make room for her stuff.

On the contrary, Dick's place is a mess. Clothes are strewn everywhere. A growing mountain of dirty dishes fills the kitchen sink. He's a slob, and he knows it. He always tells himself that he'll get his act together and become a cleaner and more organized person *after* he meets someone. Why do it before? Dick doesn't feel the need to sleep anywhere but the middle of the bed, because damn it, he bought the thing and he should enjoy all of it. "I'll move to the side of the bed when Miss Right comes along," he says to himself.

Occasionally, Tom will indulge in a silly romantic comedy, just to put himself in the right frame of mind for finding a caring, fun-loving person to be with. Occasionally, Dick watches pornography.

When Tom sees a man and woman out together, holding hands and being affectionate, he silently applauds and admires the couple, especially the man, as that is the position *he* would like to be in one day with his special someone.

When Dick sees a man and woman out together, holding hands and being affectionate, he scoffs and rolls his eyes, especially at the man, as he thinks that any guy out there with an attractive, affectionate woman by his side must be chauvinistic and manipulative.

Tom goes on dates. So far, none of the women he has met have been "the one," but he appreciates the experience and learns something every time. He keeps trying. Dick also goes on dates. When they don't work out, he says to himself, "See, I told you she wasn't the one." He's about to give up.

If you were to guess, who is going to find true love, Tom or Dick?

The answer of course is Tom. Tom has put himself into a position that will bring about the perfect woman for him. He has prepared for her.

Before he's even met her, Tom has *literally* made room for her in his life. On a daily basis, Tom puts himself in the best possible position every day, both physically (his home) and emotionally (admiring other couples, watching romantic movies, etc.).

Though Dick is lonely and wants a partner just as much as Tom, his attitude is so pervasively negative about finding a woman that he is actually *repelling* them without even realizing it. Dick must have evidence of a woman being in his life before he will make necessary changes to actually *having* a woman in his life. By viewing other men who have a quality partner as manipulative and devious, he is guaranteeing himself not to have a partner, as *he* does not want to be manipulative and devious. This, of course, is egregiously false thinking, as every man out there with a partner is not manipulative and devious, nonetheless he has lumped them all in that same category.

Tom has an enterprising mind. Dick has a negative and idle mind.

YOUR ATTITUDE DRIVES YOUR BANK ACCOUNT

Beatrice, a novice yet innovative soapmaker, wanted to start a business and came to me for some advice. I asked her what her ultimate goal was.

She literally replied with, "I don't want to be rich. I just want enough to get by. I don't want to have to mess with a huge house. That just isn't me. I couldn't deal with all that."

I was floored. This was the first thing to come out of her mouth when asked of her ultimate goal.

"Well, would you rather have a salary of $50,000 or $5,000?" I asked. I thought this was a fairly easy question to answer, and one that would reframe her mindset about earning money through her business.

She squirmed, as if I was asking a trick question.

She replied, "$5,000," peering at me carefully to see if she had answered correctly.

"Why $5,000 and not $50,000?" I asked her.

"Because I don't want to be greedy," she replied.

I said, "Can you live off of $5,000 a year?"

"No, of course not."

"Okay, then what *is* the perfect salary for you?"

"Enough to get by," she replied.

At my wits end, I said, "I'm going to need a number if you want my help."

Her shoulders sunk as her eyes rose to the ceiling. I had pinned her against a wall with some simple questions about her life's future and she completely stalled.

"I have no idea," she finally replied.

I pressed on, asking her a few more questions.

"Well, what will your company look like three years from now? Will you still be operating from home, or a different space? Who do you want your customer base to be? A wholesale distribution? Online retail? Do you want to have an employee or two by then?

She scoffed, "Oh, I'll worry about that in three years! I'm having a hard-enough time getting all my soaps made and cured for my next holiday craft show!"

Though it pains me to say, Beatrice is not an entrepreneur. At least not right now. In fact, I actually decided not to take her on as a client, as her money mentality and entrepreneurial spirit was so lacking. She had it in her to make great products, but she didn't have it in her to think big and bold, which is required of entrepreneurs. Though she may want to *be* an entrepreneur, just like Dick wants a partner in his life, the chances of her becoming successful are slim, much like Dick's chances of finding a soulmate. The underpinnings of Dick's approach to finding a soulmate are simple – he doesn't think he is worthy enough for a kind and attractive partner, so he isn't going to go out of his way to try. Similarly, Beatrice doesn't think she is worthy enough to earn a comfortable living, so she isn't going to go out of her way to decide and make a plan.

After a few more minutes of our time together, I gathered a stronger and stronger sense of her repugnance to money. She deemed wealthy people as greedy, manipulative and sinful. Beatrice had a very philanthropic heart, and seemingly aimed to give away the lion's share of any of the earnings she attained. She couldn't possibly be philanthropic *and* wealthy. She was in complete contrast. She wants to start a company, but can't stand the thought of attaining money, because in her mind, money is evil.

Stranger still is that she had been working for a company for decades, attaining a salary of about $60,000 per year. She was okay with others putting a number (and subsequent ceiling) on what she could earn, but she wasn't okay with creating a salary for *herself*. Even stranger, she couldn't even bring herself to establish a salary that at least matched what she was making at her old job!

I'd like to say that this was a bizarre case, but I actually see this weird money behavior frequently. I am convinced the reason many don't aim for wealth—or at the very least a livable wage—is from a lack of self-esteem coupled with our society's pervading sense of righteousness about having money.

JEALOUSY TOWARDS THE WEALTHY IS NORMAL

Though not a religious man, I, as previously mentioned, used to be rigorously pious and "spiritually moral" about money and wealth attainment. I was on a very large ego trip.

I was brought up in a blue-collar mentality household. We lived a meager and sustainable life. As a matter of fact, we lived on a farm in a small, tin-roofed house that burned to the ground after a lighting storm, leaving us with literally nothing but the clothes on our backs and an old car. We struggled financially. We lived like vagabonds, jumping from motel to motel, having to be given—from the kindness of others—everything from clothes to silverware to eventually a place to live. I know what it is to not have a lot of money.

Furthermore, I heard stories from my father, describing how destitute his family was. He grew up in an incredibly poor environment, and he brought that attitude with him into adulthood and fatherhood. I grew up thinking that a mindset of lack and downfall was normal, and over time I developed a completely misconstrued, negative attitude toward affluent people, even though I didn't actually *know* anyone with affluence. I was envious of them, but I cloaked my envy through a sense of righteousness and virtue. I thought virtuous people were poor and rich people were dishonorable. Over time, I assumed all wealthy people were snobby and materialistic. *Does any of this ring true with you and your upbringing?*

When talking about wealth to people who are resistant to the idea—usually based on some strange religious stance—they will often say things like, "I grew up picking cotton! I had to *really* work for my pay! I wasn't given a damn thing! I had to work for everything I have!"

They say these things with such staunch pride, never considering that wealthy people have *also* worked their asses off to get to where they are. Not only that, wealthy people are incredibly responsible with the money they worked really hard to earn.

AN INCONVENIENT TRUTH ABOUT THE WEALTHY

The overwhelming majority of millionaires in the United States came from meager backgrounds. They are NOT silver-spooners, nor are they somehow corrupt, mischievous or evil. They found a problem in the world, decided to solve it, and had the audacity and courage to risk everything for years, without ever being guaranteed a steady paycheck from anyone. Instead of earning an income by getting a job that pays them an hourly wage or salary, they decided to *create* their wealth.

Even still, the less-wealthy, envious folks I talk with will go on to complain about their lives in a way that assumes wealthier people can't relate. This could not be further from the truth, and it is an incredibly shallow point of view. Just because someone has a higher net worth than you doesn't free them from the confines of a horrible marriage, or shield them from having hemorrhoids, or having to go through cancer. Being wealthy doesn't protect them from a tragic death in the family. Being wealthy doesn't provide happiness any more than being poor does. If you think it does, you might want to really question your own depth of character.

Remember, the vast majority of millionaires in the United States are *first-generation* millionaires. That means, just like you, they also had parents from meager backgrounds who told them things like, "money doesn't grow on trees," and, "money is the root of all evil," and, "we can't afford that." They received the same money-messages that you and I did growing up. They worked the same, crummy jobs you and I did. But, they eventually got over their pious money-mentality upbringing and chose to better the world through products and services, which happened to earn them more money than most. They got out of the "Ain't it awful?" club, where everyone moans and groans about what they don't have, and instead joined a club of entrepreneurs who think big, take risks and reap rewards.

THE EYE OF THE BEHOLDER

I later asked Beatrice, "I know it is difficult for you to give me a number, as earlier you simply said, 'Enough to get by,' but if you absolutely *had* to pin down a salary, what number would that be?"

She pondered for a while, squirming in her chair. Then, I witnessed a light turn on in her mind. Seemingly through magic or divine intervention, she found her number. Her gazing eyes found mine firmly and she triumphantly stated, "I would like to earn the national average!" She was bubbling with pride. She was so satisfied with her newly-comprised answer because it placed her in the middle. Surely you can't be seen as greedy if you're in the middle of the pack, right?!

Until, of course, you simply change your perspective.

Let's take Beatrice's newfound moral-high-ground-of-a-salary and compare it to the rest of the world. The reality is, the average family income in the United States is seen as *wealth-beyond-comprehension* compared to the global majority. I've seen firsthand, people starving on the streets of Old Delhi, India. I've witnessed children, weighing no more than 40 pounds, dragging 50-pound jerry cans of water back to their family's mud hut from the only, tiny, trickling source of fresh water for miles. I've slept in the insufferable heat, humidity and grime of Port Au Prince, Haiti, with no electricity, air conditioning or water to even brush my teeth with. I've stayed in the village of Nakivumbi, which translates to, "the place of sickness and starvation," in Uganda, Africa.

But, I got to come home. I got to come back to electricity, hot water and air conditioning. I got to come back to artisan coffee, craft beer and refrigeration. I got to come home to luxury—and believe me, whether you think yourself "well off" or not, if you live in America—you are wealthy beyond comprehension compared to the vast majority of our fellow humans.

All the folks I stayed with in these countries will never experience even a *fraction* of Beatrice's devout and noble "national average" salary. You see, when simply changing the perspective to a global scale, by Beatrice's *own* definition, she would be immensely wealthy! And since she associates wealth with greed, she then must be greedy!

Beatrice's attitude about money is so small-minded and driven by her attempts to be principled that she can't think beyond what her ego tells her. She has constructed a false sense of moral high ground about money that is not only hypocritical, it is flat-out wrong.

If you look back to her very first response, you will see that she mentions not wanting a large house. She said this nonchalantly, as if having a huge home is a *requirement* of the wealthy. I was taken aback by her statement. *What a strange and unhealthy assumption to have, I thought.* She equates people with large homes as being wealthy. She also equates wealthy people as greedy. This [false] logic assumes that owning a large home means you are greedy. Since she doesn't want a large house, Beatrice must be safe from this affliction of greed.

Do you see how crazy that sounds? Who says you have to buy a bunch of stuff you don't want or need just because you have an extra zero or two in your bank account?

I mentioned that Beatrice is very philanthropic, caring deeply for the plight of others. She also associates this as somehow incongruent with being wealthy. She has made up her mind that she must have a bank account that more closely resembles Mother Theresa's or Mahatma Gandhi's than Bill Gates's. But, Bill Gates happens to be one of the biggest financial philanthropists in the world. And guess what he has a lot of?

The truth is, we all would like more money, but only some of us are actually responsible and transparent enough to admit it.

WEALTH AND MONEY ARE NOT THE SAME THING

Have you ever really considered what wealth actually means to you?

For me personally, wealth means freedom. If a family member in Texas gets sick or needs help, we can stop everything we are doing, jump in the car or grab a flight and be there. I don't have to ask for time off from a boss. I don't have to worry about my next paycheck being short. I don't have to worry about upsetting my superior and fret about it the whole trip. I can just go. That, more than anything else, is how I *personally* define wealth.

You might consider wealth to mean an annual trip to your favorite beachfront condo with the family. Or, maybe it means a loft in Manhattan. Maybe it is giving large sums of money to worthy causes. Maybe it means having the ability to take care of your parents' finances as they grow older. Wealth is what you make it. My definition of wealth is different from your definition. Your definition of wealth is different than your neighbor's. Your neighbor's definition of wealth is different from a mother of eight in Equatorial Guinea's definition of wealth. You see, wealth is a subjective construct that you get to define for yourself. It isn't a tangible object. Wealth is simply your blueprint for how to use a very simple tool, money. Furthermore, wealth is ultimately a means to an end. Tom cleared space in his closet and slept on "his" side of the bed for one simple reason. It was a means to an end. He was preparing himself for *more love in his life.*

What are you doing to prepare *more money in your life*? If wealth is a means to an end, what is your end? What are you going to do with your newfound ability to be, do and have? If you don't know, wealth is that much further away from you. If you *do* know, you can begin clearing space for it, preparing for its arrival, just like Tom has done.

POPSICLE STICKS

Imagine there was never such a thing as money. Ever. It never existed.

Now imagine that society traded popsicle sticks for all the necessities and pleasures of life. You want a cluster of bananas? That'll be two popsicle sticks. You want a new Subaru Outback? That'll run you about 250 popsicle sticks.

A woman, Lynette, who obviously knows that people need to be clean, happens to love making soap. So, she decides to start providing soap for people, and asks them if they could trade some of their popsicle sticks for the bars she makes. The more bars she makes and provides for her community, the more popsicle sticks she gets in return. She knows in her heart that if she keeps working hard, she can eventually trade in some of her popsicle sticks for a beautiful home in the mountains for her family.

Do you see how easy this concept is to grasp? Do you think Lynette is greedy and manipulative by trading soap for popsicle sticks?

Meanwhile, a fellow soapmaker, who feels holier-than-thou about attaining popsicle sticks based on their own perception of noble sensibilities, sees Lynette as money-driven and greedy. But, Lynette doesn't care about the opinions of others. She knows where her heart is. She is affording a beautiful home for her family. If someone else wants to call that greedy, so be it. She could care less. Furthermore, when being built, her house affords the construction workers with more popsicle sticks for their labor. The construction workers use raw materials to build her dream home, which provides the suppliers of the raw materials with popsicle sticks, ensuring their ability to further trade. Everyone gets popsicle sticks! It is a beautiful, reciprocal and giving model! This is the magic of business!

Having lots of popsicle sticks is not evil. Neither is having lots of money. Only one's own perception of money makes it evil. If you have a negative perception about money, you will never *have* much money. It's very simple. If you abhor the taste of broccoli, you probably aren't going out of your way to eat it. Likewise, if you believe that wealthy people are covetous and materialistic, you probably aren't going out of your way to try to obtain more money.

Or, if you *do* obtain more money—yet you haven't developed a mindset of wealth—you will quickly squander it, because your subconscious has been trained to see it as bad, therefore it doesn't want you to have it. The Certified Financial Planner Board of Standards says nearly a *third* of lottery winners eventually declare bankruptcy. They literally become financially worse off than before they became rich. Why? Because they grew up believing that money is the root of all evil, and now they have a bunch of it. So, their subconscious gets to work squandering it so they can get back into their comfort zone of lack and therefore not be burdened with the idea of being seen as greedy or evil.

Successful entrepreneurs have a good relationship with money. They can hold large sums without freaking out. They can see large sums of money in their accounts and simply appreciate it and be grateful for it. Successful people are responsible with money. They view it in the same way as Lynette viewed her popsicle sticks. Money is simply a tool you can obtain as much of or as little of as you want, and then use it to trade for physical items, experiences, events and any and all other circumstances. That's it. There isn't anything more to it than that, unless you make it some big deal.

Don't be a Dick with your money. Be a Tom. Prepare for it. Make room for it in your life. Appreciate, admire and respect those who have lots of it. Stop judging. Like Tom watching romantic comedies, engage your mind and emotions in feeling great about money in every way you can. Prepare yourself until you have such a strong sense of knowing you have it that is just starts showing up.

You can have as many popsicle sticks as you want. If people in your life shame you for your stack of popsicle sticks, you need to avoid those people, and do so quickly.

CHANGE YOUR MONEY-MESSAGES

Looking back on my life, before I took responsibility for my income, the unhappiness and increased stress I created for myself had to do with my unhealthy relationship with money. Not only was I drowning in debt, I was in a marriage with a spouse that also had a horrible relationship with money. Inevitably, we would get into recurrent, reciprocal arguments about our lack of money, which only *furthered* our lack of money.

Relating to money is every bit as important as relating to the people you care about. You need to spend time and effort to understand its implications and to find the proper place for it in your life. Money has a purpose, but only *you* create that purpose. You can responsibly govern your money, or you can have your money control you. If you allow money to control you, you will learn to hate it and despise anyone who has lots of it. Let's not do that. Let's instead learn to have a beautiful relationship with money.

What is the best way to have a beautiful relationship with money? Well, what is the best method to a great relationship in your personal life? The answer is love.

You can't enjoy a good relationship with money unless you're willing to love it, through thick and thin. Notice I didn't say to covet money or obsess over it. Coveting or obsessing over another individual will not create a beautiful relationship with them, will it? The same applies to money. Love is the answer.

Love is unconditional. Thus, our loving relationship with money must also be unconditional. When you choose to love your precious little puppy even though he completely wrecked your new couch, that is unconditional love. Or, when the patience required of you to help your child solve a problem is almost too much to bear, yet you bear it, that is unconditional love.

Unconditional love will inevitably improve relationships. It is simply the way of the world. When you give your patience, resources and energy into your most important relationships, you receive love back to you. This works with people, pets and yes, even money.

HOW DO WE DEVELOP A HEALTHY, UNCONDITIONAL LOVING BOND WITH MONEY?

1. **We pay attention to it**. When you receive a payment or any other sum into your hands or your bank account, acknowledge its presence in your life and be grateful for it.
2. **We make time for it**. Date night for couples is every bit as important as a date to make time for money in your life. You respect what you inspect. Whether you have a partner to do this with or not, carve out an hour or two every week to look at your finances, your net worth and ways to grow. Become comfortable with your money and take the time required to nurture it.
3. **We give it priority**. Most people who hate money don't know what money is. Since they don't actually know what it is, they never give it priority. As your business grows and your life

becomes even fuller, you must choose how you spend your time. Whether this is conscious or unconscious, your priorities create your value system. If you want to place more value on money in your life, you have to make a conscious choice to prioritize it. There is nothing wrong with this. Take time to look at all your finances, and do so often.

4. **We rejoice over it!** As a child, whether it was performing a guitar recital or a barrel-racing competition with my pony, I put my ribbon on the fridge for everyone to see. Mom and Dad would take me out for pizza afterwards. We celebrated my achievements. When you feel like you've made some progress with your money relationship, you must allow yourself the same moment of recognition. Be happy! It feels good, and it is a choice you get to make! Celebrate the money you have!

5. **We forgive it**. When money doesn't come soon enough, or you find yourself earning less than you hoped for at first, you need to remember that this is one blip in a relationship that literally lasts a lifetime. Forgive yourself and the circumstance that made you feel financially underappreciated and move on.

6. **We don't take ourselves so seriously**! Have you noticed that it's more fun to be around people who are willing to laugh at themselves? Those characteristics of self-awareness and the willingness to not take ourselves so seriously is a killer combination for successful relationships. *Money doesn't have to be super serious. In fact, it's better when it's not.* Remember, there is no difference between cash and popsicle sticks. Life and money should be fun. Life and money *are* fun. I love life and money! When it doesn't become fun, it is on you to improve. Humor is a great way to start the improvement process.

7. **We respect it**. An unconditional, loving relationship is built on respect for one another. Your money is always trying to tell you something, so you need to pay attention and look for the clues. Respect the money you have. Be dignified in how you handle it, and it will respond in kind.

8. **We don't blame our money for our shortcomings or bad moods**. Money is never the reason you're in a bad mood; it's your perception of the situation that causes you fear and pain. When you think you're mad at money (or lack thereof), you need to pull back the lens and try to understand how your thinking got you into this sullen place.

I love what money provides me. And I am completely unabashed about wanting more of it to further my quest to be, do and have. For me, money is just a bartering tool, a popsicle stick. It took me a long time to develop this mindset about money. For decades, I thought having money meant that I was somehow greedy and materialistic, so I repelled it. I even ran up credit cards to pay for things to further my subconscious hatred for it, which is irony in its purist form.

It's okay to like money. It's okay to want it in your life. If you want to make your soap and skin care company really work out, you must indulge in wanting a large revenue stream. It is okay. Allow it. Most importantly, stop judging yourself and others for wanting some damn popsicle sticks.

CHAPTER 3:

SUCCESS IS A DECISION

Contrary to the opinions of the majority, I do not believe success is an end result or outcome. Success is a strangely accommodating burden of a process that never truly ends. Success can sometimes feel like the most exciting moment you've ever experienced in your life. Other times success can feel mundane and normal. Other times success can be downright grueling and strenuous.

Success, much like the mindset of wealth or greed in the previous chapter, is *very* relative. As you walk down the street, you could be feeling an immense amount of success for some previous set of accomplishments. You are over the moon about a series of events that have led you to this soaring feeling of achievement. In this moment, I suppose you would be "succeeding." And in this same moment, a passerby might look at you and think to themselves, "What a bum."

I can guarantee, with no equivocation, that *my* success looks different from *your* success. And *your* success will unequivocally look different from your neighbor's success. And *this* soapmaker's success is guaranteed to look different from *that* soapmaker's success, and so on.

Thus, the first and most important thing to understand about success is that it is yours to own, if you choose. Most people go through life merely renting success. They adhere to what other people's successes appear to be, and vaguely make a plan to mimic them. They make many assumptions about success and usually falter when things get tough.

PHASES OF SUCCESS

I believe success can be broken up into five phases: 1) success is first a decision, 2) a definition, 3) a development over time. Once you have reached the developmental stage, where action is being applied daily as a means toward more success (which is defined by you), it is time to 4) assess, and either 5a) continue, or 5b) begin the process over again.

PHASE 1: MAKE THE DECISION

Success, for any of us, is a decision. We often like to think that upbringing or education or circumstances or lack of connections or unlucky breaks hold us back. Thinking that way, if nothing else, feels better because we can shift the blame elsewhere. We don't have to own it. But the blame lies squarely within us; the only things truly holding us back are the decisions we make (or don't make).

If, for example, you are overweight, it is because you have decided to be overweight, period. I know, that sounds a bit harsh. Having struggled with being a bit hefty in the past, I understand how reading that can make you feel. Indeed, there *are* external and internal circumstances, such as genetics, metabolism and glandular disorders, which can make losing weight more difficult, but the fact remains that if you consume fewer calories than what you burn, you will lose weight. This is a scientific fact.

The dedicated men and women who are physically fit *decided* to be physically fit. For them, being physically fit is the consequence of the preceding set of decisions they crafted, such as eating healthy foods, getting a gym membership, creating a fun exercise routine for themselves, meditating for five minutes every morning, stretching, etc. These are all *decisions* that turned into actions, which created the outcome of being physically fit. God, The Universe, or The Great Spirit did not bestow them with physical fitness (great genetics or not); they *made the decision*, defined what it meant for them and took action.

Conversely, a growing number of Americans have *made the decision* to be overweight. For them, being overweight is the consequence of the preceding set of decisions they crafted, such as eating unhealthy foods, not going to the gym, watching too much television, not exercising enough, etc. These are all decisions that turned into actions (or inactions), which created the outcome of being overweight. God, The Universe, or The Great Spirit did not bestow them with being overweight (poor genetics or not); they *made the decision*, defined what it meant for them and took action.

I witness many soap and skin care business owners who decide to be unsuccessful through their lack of total, 100 percent commitment, not to mention their white-knuckled grip on excuses. Many soap and skin care crafters who start their own business have a "We'll see how it goes" attitude. They leave so much to chance. They don't take 100 percent responsibility for their outcomes. Then they blame their lack of success on their location, their lack of knowing how to run a website, the price of raw materials, the lack of time they have to dedicate to their business, the current administration, the weather, just about anything. They will come up with a litany of reasons (excuses) as to why they are unsuccessful.

However, the simple, over-arching reality of their situation is that they have *decided* to be unsuccessful, and are using all of their failures as proof of their decision. Their lack of success then becomes a self-fulfilling prophecy. With every new failure, they say, "See, I told you this wouldn't work."

You are not this way. You are reading this book. You are taking action. You are deciding to be successful. Kudos!

A SUCCESS STORY: ANNE DECIDES

Anne, age 45 with two children, currently weights 200 pounds. Anne decides to lose weight. She doesn't *want* to lose weight. She *decides* to. She has made the cognitive intention to do this. Her next step then is to make a plan based on some simple questions:

- → How much weight will I lose?
- → When will I lose it?
- → What actions will I take to make this happen?

Notice the phrasing in her questions. She doesn't ask herself, "How much weight do *I want to* lose?" Rather, she asks, "How much weight *will I* lose?" Though the difference may seem subtle, it is absolutely not. Believe me.

So, Anne makes the decision to weigh 170 pounds.

It is late December, and she intends to be at her ideal weight by July 1st. She does some quick math. That is just 5 pounds a month for six months. She thinks, "Anyone can lose 5 pounds a month!"

So, in late December, Anne makes the decision to weigh 170 pounds on or before July 1st of the following year. She is currently 200 pounds, but has the resolve, fortitude and courage to [now] weigh 170 pounds. You see, Anne, in her mind's eye, is *already weighing* 170 pounds, even though the scale doesn't agree (yet). She has made the decision, with precision, accuracy and with a deadline, to weigh her ideal weight. Anne doesn't *hope to* lose weight. She isn't *wishing to* lose weight. She isn't saying, *"maybe someday I'll lose this extra weight."* She has *decided* to now live a life that creates her perfect and ideal body weight of 170 pounds.

Having decided a specific number to shoot for (170 pounds) and given herself a healthy deadline (July 1st), she then asks herself, *"How will I do this? What actions will I take to make this happen?"*

So, she starts writing every morning and every evening her ideal weight. She puts a note on the refrigerator door with her ideal target weight in big, bold letters. She decides to join a gym. She asks her new gym about personal training benefits and help. She goes to the bookstore and purchases some ideal recipe books that match her taste bud's sensibilities. For 10 minutes each day, she reads her newfound favorite health blogs. She plans her meals. She structures her week in advance, knowing when she will exercise before the week even begins. She asks her family for help and positive encouragement. She hangs out more with her physically fit friends, not to spite or discard her heavier friends, but to simply pick up on some vibes they might be sending out, as success always leaves clues. She inundates herself with her new, healthy lifestyle.

Her life blossoms in a way that she never could have imagined. Anne loses the weight and feels incredible not only physically, but mentally and emotionally. She took charge of her situation, made a decision and took action. It took time—half a year—but it was worth it. And now she has everything in place—all in the form of new, healthy habits—to continue her healthy lifestyle until her dying day.

Later that summer, at the gym, Anne strikes up a conversation with a fellow gym member. An overweight woman in her mid 40s, she tells Anne that she wishes she had a body just like Anne's. She then tells Anne that she must not have the same metabolism as Anne, and that she birthed two children, making it "virtually impossible" to lose the weight from pregnancy. She basically gives off the impression that Anne has a built-in susceptibility to being fit and healthy, and she herself is doomed to being portly. This, of course, is completely false. The fact is, Anne worked her butt off (literally) to achieve her perfect and ideal body weight. She *made the decision* and took massive action towards that decision.

You see, the chubby woman Anne strikes up a conversation with has *made the decision* to stay overweight, even though she attends the gym. Without actually knowing Anne's personal achievement towards her own health, the woman prognosticates that Anne has a predisposition to being physically fit, which is a slap in the face to Anne's success. The hefty woman was making herself feel better by falsely accusing Anne of having the luxury of already being fit and healthy.

The reality is, the overweight woman sees herself in a way that will always prevent her fitness success, unless she makes a very real cognitive decision to change. Up to this point, she has *only* made the decision to be overweight (even though she is at the gym!). Through her reasoning (excuses), she mandates to herself and anyone who will listen all the details as to why she will always remain overweight. This cycle becomes a self-fulfilling prophecy. This woman also assumed a lot about Anne, and all of her assumptions were wrong. Anne worked hard, stumbled along the way, got back up and kept going.

FAILURES ARE INEVITABLE

If Anne had the attitude of, *"We'll see how this weight-loss thing goes,"* she would never have achieved her goal. She wouldn't have harnessed the personal responsibility of her endeavor. If she had a weakened approach to her decision, she would capitulate back into her pre-decision lifestyle after the first failure.

Yes, Anne failed. A lot.

She had cheat meals. She ate cake at a party and felt bad for it. She didn't go to the gym when it was snowy outside, choosing instead to make herself a cup of sugary hot cocoa. She gave in to cravings. On a few occasions, she gorged on spicy pepperoni slices until nauseated. She gave into comfort when she knew better.

Furthermore, she had many friends and even members of her family constantly nudging her towards unhealthy decisions. These folks, who were not physically fit, did not understand what she was trying to do, nor did they empathize. They, unconsciously perhaps, did not want her to succeed at her goals because they themselves had made the decision to not be healthy.

But she kept her composure because of the resolution she made. She forgave herself for her imperfections. She climbed back in the saddle after every falter. Though she failed, she didn't equate *herself* as a failure. She had the mental fortitude to get back up and keep going. Because she *decided* and made a plan, she knew that her weight goal was simply a numbers game. All she had to do was lose 5 pounds per month for six months. If she faltered on a few meals, she would work that much harder to stay on pace.

Anne is successful because she chose to be. She succeeded in the face of several setbacks and the false opinions of others. She triumphed because of her resolve, her decision.

Remember, you are going to fail. A lot. The way in which you respond to these failures will make or break your business, literally. If you never actually make the decision to be successful, you will quit or marginalize your business after just a few setbacks, and the excuses will begin. Most people automatically find excuses and blame others when things don't work out the way they want. This seems to be particularly true in the United States, where many people buy into the myth that we are entitled to success and happiness – that someone else should be giving us what we want (as a business start-up coach, I see this in *all* age demographics, not just younger folks).

That notion makes my skin crawl. Make the decision to be successful with your business. Once you make this decision, it is time to define what that actually means for you and your company.

PHASE 2: DEFINE YOUR SUCCESS

In all my years in this beautiful industry, I've never come across a soap and skin care maker who didn't want to be successful. Everyone wants a sense of achievement in all aspects of their entrepreneurial career. Unfortunately, many never take the time and energy to define—with great specificity—what success actually means for themselves, their families and their businesses.

Remember, success is a subjective experience, meaning that defining success is entirely up to you. *It is your job.* We cannot simply all come together and comprise exactly what a successful person in our industry looks and lives like, because our own individual biases would eventually counter and object to some aspect of another's success. We cannot all be on the same page when it comes to success, because success means different things to different people.

I do not want the same success as the president of the United States of America. I do not see that form of success as something akin to my own sensibilities. I would not enjoy being the president, even though the vast majority of people across the globe would deem that prestigious achievement a success, which of course, it is. I do, however, see someone like Tim Ferris, author of, *The 4-Hour Work Week*, as a success akin to my own sensibilities. I very much like the idea of a 4-hour work week, as that is the type of success I would enjoy. Others, who are wired differently from me, might find a 4-hour work week abhorrent to their own definition of success. To each their own. Our success has to be *ours* and no one else's.

Some folks in our industry would define success as having a brick and mortar storefront in a well-traveled part of town, opening their doors to the community at large, while others might see this same scenario as too time-consuming and perhaps too expensive. In contrast, *their* definition of success might instead involve creating distinctive sales funnels through fun social media inclusion and unique branding components. Both scenarios can be deemed successful in their own right. Neither is right or wrong.

BE YOU

Because of the amount of television and social media we engage in as a society, we are consciously and unconsciously being spoon fed *other* people's ideas about success, and we fervently consume it. Then we compare ourselves to the people we see on television and social media, and we automatically deem ourselves unsuccessful by comparison. We soak up other's successful endeavors, assume we should have the same endeavors and then collapse upon our own emotional setbacks when we don't achieve on the same level. Of course, the problem with doing this is that you are walking down someone else's trail instead of blazing your own.

To first launch and then accelerate a successful soap and skin care business, you must define what *your* successful soap and skin care business actually looks like, without comparisons. Life will not grant you success through copy and paste.

WHAT DOES MY SUCCESS LOOK LIKE?

Let's engage in an exercise that will draw from you a clear definition of your own success. This exercise creates a clear vision of your ideal in the different areas of your life—of what you really want—which stems from your deepest desires, values and your life purpose.

Please keep in mind this exercise explores many different aspects of your life, not just your business. Indeed, this book is about being successful in the soap and skin care industry, but remember who you are, an entrepreneur. So, having a successful business is a means toward what end? If you do not conceptualize what having a successful business will *provide* for you and your family, you will run out of fuel along the way. It isn't enough to just define the success of your business. Go further. Go deep. Explore what your entrepreneurial success will provide the other important aspects of your life as well.

WHAT TO DO:

Start by finding a quiet, comfortable spot where you will not be disturbed. Center and focus on your breathing. If you like, put on some relaxing music.

Ask your subconscious to give you images of what your ideal life would look like if you could have it EXACTLY the way you want it in each area. After you have visualized each area and created the clear picture in your mind of the ideal, write down that vision with each area clearly defined:

- → Financial
- → Career / Business
- → Free Time / Family Time
- → Health / Appearance
- → Relationships
- → Personal
- → Community

THREE THINGS TO CONSIDER DURING THIS EXERCISE:

1. This is a practice in letting your mind really dream. This is big, magic wand thinking. Whatever you comprise in your mind's eye, you can achieve it if you work hard and smart enough. We can't hit targets we can't clearly see. Take this time to clearly "see" in your mind what each area of your life looks like if it were perfect. Take your mental handcuffs off. Don't put any restrictions on your penultimate, perfect vision of your life in all aspects. Allow yourself to think bigger than you ever have before. Remember, other people have succeeded on *enormous* scales, most of whom started with nothing. You can too, if you clearly define it. Give yourself permission to expand into boundless possibilities.

2. Be advised that this is for you, from you. You cannot visualize the well-being of others *for* them. We do not have that control, and when we try to control other's well-being, we ourselves slide backward from where we need to be on our own path. Do this exercise for you. In your visualizations, you will most likely see your loved ones, which is perfectly fine. Just be advised that you cannot visualize *their* life for them. This is about you.

3. You will be writing a lot for this exercise. If you need to take breaks, please do so. But be diligent in your clear vision. Once you close your eyes and meditate on one of the areas listed above, open your eyes and write down in vivid detail your vision of said area, and do so in the present tense.

THE PRESENT TENSE!

That means you DO NOT use phrases like, "I want…, Maybe someday…, I wish…, I hope…" Phrasing your decisions this way is not a decision at all. It is just wishful thinking, and that isn't good enough. Write it down in the present tense, *as if it were all happening right now, today.* The way in which I phrase each of my visions is by starting the sentence with, "I am so grateful now that…"

PHASE 3: DEVELOP YOUR SUCCESS

After Anne made the decision to lose weight and be healthy (Phase 1), she then clarified it by stating her target weight with a deadline (Phase 2). Then she joined a gym. She learned something new every day on her favorite health blog. She took nightly walks with her family. She obtained and actualized healthy recipes. Anne took a massive amount of action to reach her goal, which is Phase 3:

Developing your success, is about taking action. Massive action.

Without first deciding on, and then defining what success looks like for you and your family, taking action might be moot. Sure, you might be productive, but productivity for the sake of doing something doesn't necessarily contribute to the advancement of your company. Being very intentional in the actions you take toward the success you seek is vital.

BERNIE TAKES ACTION

Bernie decides to build a successful soap and skin care company. He takes 100 percent responsibility for the outcome of his newfound business. It is firmly established in his mind and body that his company is successful (Phase 1).

Bernie then proceeds to define what his successful company will look and feel like (Phase 2):

Bernie doesn't mind working long hours. In fact, he thoroughly enjoys it. So, he decides that working **50-60** hours a week on his business is a part of the successful process he will undertake. For him, 50-60 hours a week is a great definition of success, as he is a busybody and thoroughly enjoys the workload.

Bernie knows that he isn't much of a salesman, and he doesn't want to learn how to be one. He'd rather focus on product development and branding. So, hiring a sales person to represent his company is another part of the successful process he will undertake. Delegating tasks is incorporated into his definition of success.

Bernie enjoys learning about website building, so having a strong online retail presence is yet another part of the successful process he will undertake. He knows that he would rather not have a brick and mortar store, so he continues to define the outlook of his company accordingly. He has defined his company's success as an online retail center.

Bernie continues to define all other aspects of his company's success, down to the most minute detail. He knows exactly how much the company will generate in total sales, what his salary will be, his overheads, the amount of taxes he will owe, the color scheme of his logo and website, his product packaging, the fonts he wishes to use on all marketing materials, his different streams of revenue, the amount of capital it will take to achieve the necessary economies of scale for low-cost manufacturing, etc. His definition of success is incredibly clear and vivid.

Because he has such a clear vision as to what his company now looks like, Bernie can take massive daily action towards the manifestation of his decided success (Phase 3):

Generally speaking, every piece of appropriate action towards a larger goal should be written down. For Bernie's company, having a strong online presence with ever-growing visitor traffic requires that he be present and interactive with his online customer base. To do this, he decides to create a series of blog posts on his website to keep people in tune with his company's activities. Ever the planner, Bernie decides to come up with 52 different blog post ideas for his new website, as there are 52 weeks in a year. It takes him about an hour to strum up 52 different topics. Next, on a calendar, he writes down the perfect blog topic idea for each of the 52 weeks in the year. He makes sure his blog post ideas match up with the appropriate time of the year. His pumpkin spiced product blog post will be in October, his gardening-product focused blog post shall be in May, etc. Placing each blog post topic in the appropriate calendar spot took about an hour.

Now he has a 52-part online marketing plan on his calendar for the upcoming year. The next thing he does is dedicate eight hours a week over the next three weeks to complete all 52 blog posts. His plan is to have them—all 52—completed *before* the upcoming year begins. He breaks down his 24 hours (eight hours per week for the next three weeks) of total effort towards this accomplishment by dividing his time allotment by 52 blog posts.

The three weeks pass and Bernie now has 52 completed blog posts for his new website. All he has to do is publish one per week to have a recurrent presence in the online community with his customers and potential buyers for the *entire upcoming year*.

Here is the breakdown in hours:

→ One hour to make the list of 52 blog post topics

→ One hour to place each blog post topic in the appropriate calendar spot

→ Twenty-four hours to complete all blog posts

Thus, in 26 total hours, Bernie has completed an incredible amount of work that will set the entire online-presence faction of his business for an entire year. Bernie took *massive action*. What if you did this with all aspects of your business? What if you did this with all aspects of your *life*?

And if 26 hours of work dedicated to only one faction of your business over a 3-week period seems like too much, you are in the wrong line of work. To put it in perspective, the average American watches about four and a half hours of television per day. In three weeks, that would be 94.5 hours of television, or almost *four entire days*. If, up to this point in your life and business, your priorities fall in line with the national average of television time, you have probably not decided, defined nor taken massive action toward the type of success that our friend Bernie has.

MASSIVE ACTION

Define what success looks like in all aspects (departments) of your business. Write it all down. Make a list of to-dos on paper, and give each of them a clear deadline. Then take clear, massive action to complete your list, one by one. Chunk down big goals into weekly, daily, hourly tasks, just like Bernie did.

And remember, you can't take serious and dedicated action without first deciding and then defining what you are going for. Every action is a means to an end. Make sure that end is *exactly* what you want.

PHASE 4: ASSESS YOUR SUCCESS

In the first paragraph of this chapter, I offered up the idea that success can sometimes feel like the most exciting moment you've ever experienced in your life, while other times it can feel mundane and normal. And still other times it can feel downright grueling. Allow me to explain this through my own experience by first giving you the background (Phases 1-3) and then showcasing what it means to assess (Phase 4).

PRAIRIE SOAP COMPANY, LLC: PHASE 1 (DECIDE)

During the early, primary stages of my business, Prairie Soap Company LLC, I developed a strong commitment to succeed. I made the decision to be successful, no matter the odds, no matter the risk. I was a successful entrepreneur, period. That is how it was going to be. It was the late summer of 2009.

PRAIRIE SOAP COMPANY, LLC: PHASE 2 (DEFINE)

I began to clearly define what Prairie Soap Company's success actually meant to the business entity, me, my business partners, employees, customers, community, our future, my financial earnings, our literal presence and establishment...everything I could possibly think of (literally *none* of which I had actually obtained yet). I wrote everything down in the positive, present tense. I followed the rules from the action exercise earlier in this chapter. I wrote out my perfect story with vivid detail, as if it were happening at the very moment I was writing it.

In this vivid detail came the idea of a retail storefront. My mother, Sheila, also my business partner, had always wanted a retail storefront to share with our community, and I very much wanted the same. So, together, we began writing in crystal clarity what our store would look and feel like. We decided on the paint on the walls, all the products we would offer, all the customers we would have, the gatherings we would sponsor to bring our community together…again, all written in the positive, present tense. This action-oriented visualization exercise became so solid in our minds that we *knew* we were to have it someday. We had made a firm decision that this would come about, and nothing was going to stop us.

PRAIRIE SOAP COMPANY, LLC: PHASE 3 (DEVELOP)

For three long and arduous years, we worked day in and day out on our business. We built up our economies of scale to the point of mixing, pouring and cutting thousands of bars a week. We had established wholesale accounts across the country and a gradually-growing presence online. We were hitting our goals, paying all the overheads and putting money in our pockets. We still didn't have our storefront, but we never lost faith in the process. We knew the decision was made and it was just a matter of time.

One day out of the blue, I received a call from a retail outlet leasing agency. They wanted to know if we were interested in opening a temporary, "pop-up" style storefront for the upcoming holiday season. It was the late summer of 2012. After some back and forth, we decided to do it.

We now had the storefront we had always dreamed of!

We worked so hard on putting together a truly unique, inviting and beautiful retail storefront that would establish a strong sense of belonging with our community, that the leasing agency asked us to stay longer. And then longer still. This, of course, was all part of our plan. We made the decision to wow them with our company, and it worked.

So, we officially had reached our goal. For the ensuing years, we indeed built a strong sense of belonging with our community. We put our heart and soul into our store. Word got out. We were a beloved local feature in a sea of big box chain stores. Everything we had written down in crystal clear detail had come to pass. Literally. Our plan on paper was accurately manifesting itself day by day. I was having the time of my life, and we were making great money.

PRAIRIE SOAP COMPANY, LLC: PHASE 4 (ASSESS)

As the years went by, our company's profits continued to grow and I learned much along the way about how to make better decisions that led to greater profit, explained in my book, *Pricing Handmade Soap for Profit*.

I was content in my store. We were still catering to all of our wholesale accounts and recurrently landing new ones. We taught soapmaking classes every Saturday. I had employees and a sales rep to help me with the heavy lifting of the business. My main focus was on accounting and new product development.

Three to four years prior to this point in my life and career, I had first made the decision to be successful, and then laid out a crystal-clear plan on how I would get there. What I was now doing, day in and day out, was the manifestation of what I had written. I was literally living my dream.

Alas, my living dream eventually became mundane.

I admit it. Call me petty, but after achieving this personal and professional milestone, I was feeling pretty humdrum about all the routines, chores and responsibilities I was encumbered with over the years. Don't get me wrong, I was emphatically grateful for my circumstance, expressing immense appreciation for my success through journaling, prayer, contemplation and general conversation. But, the feelings of monotony were growing ever present in my life and work. I was burned out. I am a person who *loves* change. I always have been, always will be. My entrepreneurial efforts and work situation did not permit me to experience a lot of change, which eventually became an emotional snag.

Through the eyes of all my fellow soapmaking peers, I was looked upon as a success. Many expressed appreciation and were encouraged by my progress as a soapmaking entrepreneur. They told me how amazing it must be, and how accomplished I must feel. But the truth was, the level of success I had achieved felt monotonous and normal. I wasn't having as much fun as when we first reached this new milestone, when it was new.

This is why I so emphatically explain that success is relative. I reached the achievement that many of my peers were striving for, and eventually, all I wanted was to get out of my situation. In this instance, my definition of success was needing to change, while many of my peer's definition of success was the thing I was doing every day. You see, success is a relative, subjective experience, not to mention a finicky little bugger.

Around this time, I met a young woman named Amanda. She was building a 501(c)3 not-for-profit organization, The Lovin' Soap Project, wherein she was to travel to developing nations and teach groups of women how to make soap from local, sustainable materials as a means of empowerment.

Through a series of remarkable events, Amanda asked me to go to Haiti with her to teach (My company had donated to her cause, which is how she knew who I was, though we didn't actually *know* each other). I agreed, and just a few months later we were teaching a wonderful group of women how to make soap in a small village on the southern coast of Haiti. We developed a strong rapport with each other as the workshops carried on, which propelled Amanda to ask if I would join her as co-director of the organization. I wholeheartedly agreed.

We recurrently traveled back to Haiti, often just for three or four days at a time, as that was all my schedule would allow. I developed such a fondness for the project that it was all I could think about. I engaged myself so deeply into our new budding organization that my own business, Prairie Soap Company, was quickly becoming marginalized.

IT WAS TIME TO ASSESS MY SUCCESS

After just a few months of marketing and fundraising for the project, we were being asked to travel all over the world to teach. We had opportunities to go to sub-Saharan Africa, India, Tibet and more. There was no way I could possibly work on both my company and our non-for-profit on a fulltime scale. Running a company that hosts a storefront, supplies goods to retail outlets all over the country and has a presence online demands a 100 percent time, energy and resource commitment. I knew, after assessing my situation, that I needed to make a change. I wanted to commit myself to the Lovin' Soap Project. I wanted to travel the world. I wanted to help change lives through empowerment. This was my new decision. This was my *new* definition of success.

So, we closed the doors to the store, even after our most financially successful year to date. I began recurrently traveling to Uganda, Tibet, India, Fiji and Senegal. This was my new definition of success. I was manifesting a new, beautiful dream of empowerment and wonder. I reached a new, subjective level of success that some couldn't possibly understand, which is perfectly fine. Later, Amanda and I got married.

CHANGE IS INEVITABLE

Fortunately for me, change comes easy. I guess it's just the way I'm wired. I don't mind it, I even thrive during change. That said, I know that change can be difficult for many.

But, if we as entrepreneurs don't learn to embrace change and move forward, we will be left behind or worse, be unhappy. So, whether it's changing the focus of your business, having to learn new technology or replacing a prized employee, you need to know how to deal with change. And really, that is what assessment is all about – the willingness to candidly see what needs to change, and when it is time to change. Stagnation can really muddy things up.

HOW TO ASSESS

It is crucial to both completely separate your personal assessment from your business assessment, and at the same time delicately mingle them together with as much objectivity as possible. You are not your business, and your business is not you. While assessing your business and yourself, do so individually and on their own merit, and then go back and fuse them together to see if they concur in a unified manner.

BUSINESS ASSESSMENT

A business assessment is pretty simple. Simply ask yourself and your team a few questions:

- → Is the business profitable?
    - → If so, how do we further capitalize?
    - → If not, how do we reduce our expenses and create profit?
- → If we are not currently profitable, are we equipped—mentally, physically and emotionally—to create profit in the foreseeable future?
- → What do we need to know that we currently do not know?
    - → What steps can we take to learn?
- → What is currently working for us?
- → What is not working for us?
- → What should we be doing more of?
- → What should we be doing less of?

- → Are all of our products successful? Is there one or two that we can cut from our product line that will create better chances of overall profit?

- → Are we marketing enough?

- → Do we have a strong brand?

    - → *Do we know how to brand?*

- → What are we doing to promote, advertise and market?

    - → *Do we know how to promote, advertise and market?*

- → What does our business look like in one year?

    - → Is this vision good enough for us? Could it be better?

- → Do we have clear goals?

    - → Are our goals stretching us?

PERSONAL ASSESSMENT

- → Do I love doing this? Do I love my company?

    - → If so, what exactly do I love about this business?

    - → If not, why?

- → What are my biggest strengths with this business?

- → What are my biggest weaknesses with this business?

    - → Do I have what it takes to learn what I do not currently know so that I may grow my business? If not, can I delegate?

- → Do I know—deeply and completely—what profitability really means?
- → Is this taking too much of my time, energy and resources?
- → How long do I want to do this?
- → Am I willing to sacrifice and squeeze out a small salary until my company grows?
- → Are there any aspects of my business that I can't stand?
  - → If so, list them. Can you dump any of them? Delegate to someone else?
- → When I think about my company, does it drain me or excite me?

REFLECTING IS GOOD FOR THE SOUL

Without assessing my business and myself, I would have never taken the leap that I did into the unknown, co-founding and co-directing a not-for-profit organization that allows me to travel the world, meet new and wonderful people and empower. If I had played it safe, I would have stayed where I was, as I knew we were profitable, I had a healthy salary and our company was steadily growing. But, after assessing, I knew I needed to change and grow. After assessing, I became calm about the entire closing process. The actual procedure of assessing my life and my business relaxed me to the point where I was embracing this newfound grasp on my career with fervor and excitement. I was ready to move on, which leads me to Phase 5.

PHASE 5: CONTINUE OR START OVER

Speaking as objectively as possible, my decision to begin again on a new journey was not necessarily a *better* decision than if I were to have stayed in my store and continued doing what I was doing. If I had stayed, I would have simply continued on, perhaps steadily seeking out new profit goals, new product development and acquired more wholesale accounts. But, I chose to start over.

Starting over is just that. I had a new endeavor, The Lovin' Soap Project. I had a brand-new life and career to define and create for myself. So, I went back to Phase 1. I decided that this newfound approach to a life and career was going to be successful.

I re-wrote my vision, including all aspects of what it would be like as a traveling, rambling man. I wrote down all the places I intended to visit, many of which I am proud to say I now have. I was crystal clear in how I wanted the project to grow through funding. I inundated myself in everything I wanted to move forward with. I inundated myself in Phase 2.

Phase 3 was simple. We acted on our intentions from Phase 2. I traveled, taught, raised money, traveled, taught, raised money, etc.

And so, the cycle continues. I constantly assess my situation, looking for modifications both personally and professionally. We are growing our not-for-profit organization to take on new teachers because of our plans to make a family. We know we will be out a few months or so to take care of a newborn, so we assessed, made a new plan and hired new people to continue our project. Assessment is constant.

Everything clicks when you have a vision towards your own success. The Universe just seems to work with you, in conjunction, to co-create what it is you are seeking. But, I strongly believe that we cannot use the Universe's co-creative efforts if we don't have a clear and unique vision on paper.

RAISING THE BAR

Remember, success is not an end result or outcome. It is an ever-changing process that demands your crystal-clear vision and intentions. When we set the bar for our companies and ourselves, and then actually reach the bar, we typically don't relish it for very long before we raise the bar again. This is what entrepreneurialism is all about – always raising the bar.

Take the time you need to create your life and business on paper, make a plan and assess as you proceed down your own unique path. Owning a soap and skin care business should be fun. When it doesn't give you fun anymore, that doesn't mean you have to quit. It means you have to assess where you and your company are, respectively. Perhaps there is a glimmer for a new project, a new product line or a new, crazy way to garner more customers. Maybe you have the wrong company name, and you need to completely rebrand. Though that may sound daunting, it might be a very fun undertaking. Maybe assessing your packaging has led you to commence a new, vibrant look that better suits your company's look and feel. Whatever it may be, take the time to assess your company's weaknesses and where you, the head of the company, participate in those weaknesses.

You have to be really honest with yourself throughout these five phases of success in order for it to work for you. Your ideas will lay dormant unless you open yourself up to recurrently changing decisions and definitions of success.

CHAPTER 4:
MISSION, VISION & VALUES

Developing an overarching company mission, vision and set of values is not something to be left only to big corporations. It isn't some commercialized mumbo-jumbo. It is important to have a company mission. Your business must have a north star. You must have a direction, with clear trail markers along the way, indicating that you are on the right path. Don't underestimate the importance of a solid mission and mission statement. Every entrepreneur should write a mission statement early on, as they provide you, your employees, friends and family with framework and purpose.

MISSION, VISION & VALUES: 4 QUESTIONS

1. **What do we do?**

If you answer this question like a C average high-schooler doing the bare minimum on their homework assignment, you would answer with something like, "I make soap."

That is true, but way too bland and generic. No emotion, no power. Give me something more. Allow me to give you an example:

> "At Earth & Salt Soapworks, we handcraft the finest quality soap and skin care products in small batches, utilizing the abundant qualities of natural oils from all over our planet."

2. **How do we do it?**

> "Earth & Salt Soapworks utilizes an ancient technique to craft natural soaps, referred to as 'cold-process.' Our process employs an aging progression with each soap we create, allowing them to cure for six weeks on solid oak racks.
>
> We procure our exotic salts, utilized in our scrubs and soaks, directly from the Dead Sea, which is sheltered in the middle of two ancient nations: Israel and Jordan. Various cultures and groups of people have visited the Dead Sea for therapy dating back to the ancient Egyptians."

See what I did? The reality is, your soap curing on four by eight-foot oak boards from Home Depot doesn't sound that appealing or special, nor does it contribute anything to the soap. *But it sounds good, right?* And even though you are up to your earholes in soapmaking jargon, remember that your customers are not, so they probably do not know what cold-process means. So, entice them (and yourself, and your employees (future or present)) by showcasing a simple, yet profound fact: the process has been around for a very long time! The same applies if you are a hot-processer. Be proud of what you know and understand about what you create. You are an artist *and* a scientist! Embrace it!

Furthermore, we incorporated history and geography into bath soaks! Think big! Be bold! What senses can you invoke through your message? We have only five of them, so surely you can incorporate at least a couple.

3. **For Whom do we do it?**

This is the money shot question, and you must provide a meaningful and genuine answer in the form of powerful statements.

> *"Earth & Salt Soapworks was created for people who care just as much about their 'external' nourishment as their 'internal' sustenance.*
>
> *To be fully nurtured is to care deeply for not only our largest organ, but the one that is in endless contact with the outside world, our skin. Our bodies have a vitality and message for the world if we listen.*
>
> *Earth & Salt Soapworks was built for the nourishment and safekeeping of your temple, your body."*

4. **What value are we bringing?**

With any products-based business, real, concrete value should be both consistency and predictability. One of the main reasons the Chipotle franchise has done so well over the years is due to their consistency and predictability. Everyone knows *exactly* what they are going to get before they even get in line, and they know *exactly* how it is supposed to taste.

Your soap and skin care company is no different. From the overall messages, packaging, shipping method, website experience, etc., your company should be consistent, dependable and predictable. The Lavender Lemon soap bar you craft in 2017 should have the exact same consistency and predictability as the one you craft in 2030. This is the *tangible* side to value.

The *intangible* side of value in your soap and skin care company should be derived from your ultimate vision. Where do you want to take your company, and why? What greater good are you providing the world? What immaterial (as opposed to 'material,' i.e. soap or other body product) value can your company provide?

> *"Earth & Salt Soapworks is a self-sustaining company that provides exemplary products for the mind, body and soul. Our products are derived from premium ingredients, Earth-friendly packaging and a commitment to quality and global outreach. Your experience with us creates a shared sense of belonging to the greater community, furthering our commitment to society at large. It is our promise to always practice the importance of people over profits."*

Combining the answers to all four questions above creates a beautiful mission, vision and set of values that this made-up company can hang its hat on.

You should feel a sense of pride and motivation after reading your mission, vision and values. You should feel a sense of forward motion. If you do not, your message isn't good enough. If it isn't good enough for you, it won't be good enough for your customers. They will see right through it.

Making great soap and skin care products is easy. All seven billion people on the planet can learn how to make great soap. So, what sets your company apart? The answer is ultimately in your mission, vision, values and the way in which you convey these messages to your customer.

Look at how these heartfelt example answers might be perceived on an *About Us* page on a beautifully designed website:

Our Mission:

> *At Earth & Salt Soapworks, we handcraft the finest quality soap and skin care products in small batches, utilizing the abundant qualities of natural oils from all over our planet.*

Our Products:

> *Earth & Salt Soapworks utilizes an ancient technique to craft natural soaps, referred to as 'cold-process.' Our process employs an aging progression with each soap we*

create, allowing them to cure for six weeks on solid oak racks.

We procure our exotic salts, utilized in our scrubs and soaks, directly from the Dead Sea, which is sheltered in the middle of two ancient nations: Israel and Jordan. Various cultures and groups of people have visited the Dead Sea for therapy dating back to the ancient Egyptians.

Our Community:

Earth & Salt Soapworks was created for people who care just as much about their 'external' nourishment as their 'internal' sustenance.

To be fully nurtured is to care deeply for not only our largest organ, but the one that is in endless contact with the outside world, our skin. Our bodies have a vitality and message for the world if we listen.

Earth & Salt Soapworks was built for the nourishment and safekeeping of your temple, your body.

Our Vision:

Earth & Salt Soapworks is a self-sustaining company that provides exemplary products for the mind, body and soul. Our products are derived from premium ingredients,

> *Earth-friendly packaging and a commitment to quality and global outreach. Your experience with us creates a shared sense of belonging to the greater community, furthering our commitment to society at large. It is our promise to always practice the importance of people over profits.*

From these messages, I can see in my mind's eye a color palette for labels, fonts for packaging and website, and even a logo. I can visualize how the website will look, and even the product photography. I even have ideas on product names, and how they will be showcased with quality product descriptions. Most importantly, I know *exactly* who my customers will be. And though my mental visual of this might be different from yours, as creativity is subjective, I am willing to bet you can see your own version of this pretend company as well. The company message should stimulate the mind and stir emotion.

Do you see how this is starting to work? Do you see the importance of doing this?

If not, allow me to explain:

Most soap and skin care business owners just start making and selling, which of course is encouraged, but only to a degree. They become rather hasty about naming their company, not thinking through a quality, polished logo and impulsively throwing together whatever the cheapest, DIY packaging and labels they can come up with. They can't project past the next upcoming craft show to see the bigger picture of what their company's true potential is. Their company's color schemes are all over the place, and they use seven different typographies on their various marketing materials and website. There is no cohesion, *because there is no foundational mission.*

They hope their products will sell based on the merit of the ingredients and the formulating process. Their company has no semblance of a story, an overarching mission with goals, nothing. They just make great soap and skin care products, and they hope it sells wherever and whenever and to whomever. This is what I call hope marketing. You make a great product and then hope it sells.

You must have a strong mission, vision for the future and set of values that your company lives and breathes by. Crafting your company's mission and message (intangible value) first will *open the door* to your company name, color schemes, fonts, logo, tagline, product packaging, product descriptions, etc. (mainly, tangible value).

Allow me to engage you further still to sledgehammer my point through some examples of *not* making a plan that includes a mission, vision and set of values:

→ You hastily launch a soap and skin care company—with no mission, vision or values—and name the company, "Lisa's Lovely Lather," which, by the way, is perfectly fine. But, you then create a men's product line, which doesn't sell, and you wonder why. Of course, the "why" behind the men's product line not selling is most likely due to the name of the company. "Lisa's Lovely Lather" is very female driven, certainly not a bad thing, but might feel inauthentic when it comes to making and selling men's products. If you had first set up a very genuine and transparent mission, vision and values from the start, you might have avoided this.

→ You hastily launch a soap and skin care company—with no mission, vision or values—and declare your business to be as natural and sustainable as possible by any set of market standards. You then use plastic wrap, a petroleum byproduct, to package all your soaps, and customers become appalled by the obvious disconnect between your company's claims of being natural and sustainable and using plastics when there are more natural alternatives. If you had first set up a very genuine and transparent mission, vision and values from the start, and then asked yourself if plastic packaging fell in line with your company's values, you might have avoided this. Obviously, there is nothing wrong with using plastic wrap as long as it fits into your company's greater set of values.

→ You hastily launch a soap and skin care company—with no mission, vision or values—and decide to use the logo-design expertise of your neighbor's 14-year old daughter. The budding artist, whom you love dearly, constructs a logo that leaves something (or many things) to be desired, but you feel compelled to use it so that you don't hurt feelings. You are now stuck with an inferior logo, which aesthetically sets the stage for *everything* your company does moving forward. If you had first set up a very genuine and transparent mission, vision and values from the start, you might have avoided this by knowing exactly what you wanted and then taken your idea to a professional, knowing that your ultimate vision required it.

Don't approach writing your company's mission, vision and values as if it were some obligatory assignment. If you do, you might want to consider how dedicated you really are to all of this in the first place. If you really take the devoted time and energy, in a quiet setting, with solitude and an open heart, you will be able to convey a strong and sincere message. Put your phone away. Turn the television off. Create a positive, serene environment in which to think and visualize. Then start writing. You won't get it perfect on your first try. You can always polish it later. Just focus on pouring your heart and soul into your company's mission, vision and values, and leave the refining to a later date. Take the dedicated time and energy to create a strong company message. Make this the foundation of everything you are to build moving forward.

By wholeheartedly completing a well-thought-out set of mission, vision and values, you will have identified clear, measurable and demonstrable benefits consumers get when buying your company's products. Done effectively, you will now be able to convince consumers that your products are better than others on the market. The proposition you will have written can lead to a competitive advantage when consumers pick your particular products over other competitors, because they know they will receive greater value, both tangible and intangible.

CHAPTER 5:

STYLE MATTERS

After creating a mission statement with a set of worthy values and a clear vision to move your company forward, I'm willing to bet that you have unearthed a certain style—a source of expression—from which you would like to convey your foundational messages.

In the consumer-driven developed world, we no longer want just the utility of the products we buy. We want the experience. We want to soak up the style that a company is showcasing to us. The style and flavor of how you furnish your messages, visual aesthetics, marketing materials, logo, language and product packaging is just as important as the coconut oil you use. Like it or not, we are fickle creatures, especially in the developed world, where we get to pick and choose our experiences without dire consequence. *Customers in the developed world already have their basic needs met from the perspective of functionality. What they seek most from you is for their aesthetic needs to be met.*

FROM MORNING FUEL TO MOUTHWATERING EXPERIENCE

Do you remember when having a cup of coffee was not a cultural necessity? Do you remember when Folgers and Maxwell House took the lion's share of the caffeinated bean market?

I started drinking coffee when I was 18 years old, a senior in high school. And probably much like many who read this book, I grew up on the commodity-driven, mass-produced brand of Folgers. I didn't really know the diversity of coffee roasters out there, primarily because they *weren't* really out there. As a young adult in the early 2000s, the internet wasn't like it is today. Phones weren't socially mandatory, and the corporate giants in products-based businesses still ruled their respective industries without "little" companies getting in the way.

Starbucks changed everything.

I can still remember my first cup of Starbucks coffee. I remember the smell wafting through the air as I walked into the shop. All the merchandise was enveloped in a colorful, bohemian exposition, with the iconic mermaid logo strategically placed. Customers were sipping their lattes and mochas while reading books and scampering their fingers across their laptops on comfortable chairs. I ordered a large ('venti') coffee.

I had never tasted something so good. You must remember, I knew nothing other than Folgers. I assumed that the brackish, bitter grounds from the big plastic red tub was how coffee was supposed to taste. My maiden cup from Starbucks changed everything. I could actually taste a rich, balanced flavor. I could taste subtle notes of cocoa and toasted nuts. The difference was not apples and oranges – it was apples and giraffes. As an avid coffee drinker, I was in heaven.

Not long after, I started seeing Starbucks coffee offered in grocery stores and specialty shops in beautifully branded foil bags with a tiny hole in the front, allowing me to gently squeeze the bag and waft what was inside. The artful, sophisticated look of the coffee bag with its built-in enticement nose-hole was too much for me to resist. Of course, Starbucks was much more expensive than my timeworn Folgers brand, but that didn't matter. I started paying 40 – 50 percent more for my coffee without ever thinking about it. And you know what? I felt really good about myself when I made the switch. I was now part of a new, cultured segment of society who respected a product for its quality and pleasure, instead of just using it as a means to wake up in the morning.

STARBUCKS DIDN'T JUST SELL ME COFFEE.

THEY SOLD ME AN EXPERIENCE.

Customers don't just want fuel. They want pleasure — quality offerings in an aesthetically appealing environment. They want convenience, but not by foregoing quality. They want to feel good about themselves because of the purchase they just made. Customers want to be able to feel a sense of pride and inclusion in a purchase, not complacency. Most of all, especially when it comes to the artisan market, customers *never* want to feel normal, plain or mundane. They want to be made to feel exceptional.

The look and feel of a product and the experience customers go through to purchase, increasingly drives economic value. Businesses today face an aesthetic imperative. **Style can no longer be an afterthought.** It has become a critical source of product identity and economic value. The desire for interesting, enjoyable, and meaningful sensory experiences is everywhere, and that will never, ever go away. Yes, Starbucks is a better-quality coffee than Folgers, but product-quality is only a small part of their marketing. Starbucks created an experience through beautiful aesthetics that urged a sense of inclusion.

Today, ironically enough, I rarely purchase anything from Starbucks. I have switched my roasted bean loyalties to a few other dedicated, artful brands that appeal to me even more. But, Starbucks paved the way for the coffee brands I now enjoy. They made every piece of the experience matter. Starbucks is the foundation to an escalating cottage industry in a global market.

Starbucks never tried to compete with Folgers on price. They couldn't. The sourcing of their beans, along with their branding and marketing messages simply cost too much. They charged higher prices based on aesthetic imperative. They knew that a large percentage of customers would never buy their product, and they were perfectly fine with that.

Sure, every business wants more customers, but if Starbucks had cast a huge net with their offerings and didn't create a pleasing and aesthetic environment, they would have failed. They are fancy coffee and they are proud of it.

Through their mission, vision, values and visual appeal, they *created* a customer base. Now, it would seem, everyone in the world knows Starbucks. They know the green-colored mermaid. They know Pike's Peak is not just a mountain. They have become globally recognized.

Starbucks did it. Why can't you?

ABSOLUT

In a global market absolutely dominated by Russia, a vodka startup from Sweden decided to get a piece of the action. Many "experts" advised against it. Ten years after they entered the market, they were one of the hottest-selling vodkas in the United States, and have since grown their global market share substantially.

They did NOT achieve this success through product quality, efficient distribution or price. They are considered a *middle-of-the-road* vodka based on taste, their distribution logistics were no different from other spirit distilleries, and they are stationed somewhere in the middle of the market on price. So how did they garner such a large share of the marketplace so quickly?

They had a willingness to market style. They knew about the aesthetic imperative. So, Absolut created a style that portrayed:

- → Smart
- → Showy
- → Sassy
- → Sophisticated
- → Sometimes silly
- → Always trendy

Their distinctly shaped bottle—actually an older, clear medicine bottle—is cleverly combined with the strong (yet minimal), royal blue words, ABSOLUT VODKA spelled across. The color blue denotes trust, which is what Absolut—in combination with a dedication towards style—needed to build their brand. The bottle was topped with a polished silver cap, which when combined with the traditional clear bottle and royal blue letters kept with their overall panache. Absolut was streamlined, straightforward and sophisticated, not to mention very clean and crisp in its appearance, which happens to be what vodka drinkers are looking for in taste.

Much like beauty, style is in the eye of the beholder. So, who is deeming this chic bottle of spirits stylish?

Absolut targeted the ever-growing crowd of hip, creative folks who seek a high-end culture, namely cosmopolitans, metrosexuals and fashion-enthusiasts. Of course, Absolut is too smart to just market their stylish vodka to folks who are already stylish. Absolut marketed their style to *people who wanted to be a part of this stylish culture*. There are far more people who *want* to be in the scene than who *are* in the scene. That's what makes the scene cool, right? Absolut knew this. This was their genius.

ICED TEA

Iced tea without ice is just tea. You must have *both* items to call it iced tea. If the ice is your customer base, and the tea is your business, they together form your brand. Without your customers (ice), all you have is a business (tea) – and that isn't enough. Building a soap *business* is easy. Building a soap *brand* is far more involved.

Furthermore, not all ice is the same. Some ice comes as huge cubes. Some are smaller and more cylindrical. Some ice is crushed. To really have the perfect glass of iced tea, you need the perfect ice to go with it, right? That is, your customer base (ice) must be unique to your business (tea) to make the perfect brand (delicious iced tea).

Attempting to be all things to all people never works. This method is an obvious sign of an underdeveloped or nonexistent brand. You must choose a set of people that will match up to your company's overall mission and message. You must choose the perfect ice for your iced tea (or vodka!).

BRANDING A BUSINESS IS BRANDING A CUSTOMER

I believe your brand is ultimately defined by your customer's overall perception of your company. It isn't defined by everyone out there; it is defined by your specific, targeted customer. Thus, we are left with a bit of a chicken-or-egg scenario. Since your brand is defined by your specific customer's *perception* of your business, who comes first – your brand or your specific customer?

The answer is both. We must play up the brand to our specific customer, and we must play up the customer to our specific brand. It is a delicate balance between projecting (out) your message and pulling (in) people to your business through emotion.

To reiterate, neither Absolut's actual product, nor its service quality, nor its excellent operations and financial management can explain Absolut's success (although these obviously play a vital role). Absolut differentiated itself from the more traditional, stoic styles of well-founded vodka brands with a new, modern style that greatly appealed to a younger, trendy demographic. They didn't take the traditional "style path" of Russian or American vodkas. Absolut pioneered a new style simply by its aesthetic messages.

WHAT IS STYLE?

In the context of creating a company "style," I would define it as a distinctive manner of expression. It isn't just *what* you say, it is *how* you say it. Think about the difference in style between two companies that offer the exact same products and services – insurance.

Allstate Insurance has a very enduring style, their logo a welcoming pair of hands that are cupped in a way that implies a sense of providing. Allstate's style is to be a caregiver, with their tagline being, "You're in good hands."

Now let's look at Progressive Insurance. I dare say anyone reading this book who doesn't know Flo, the quirky, approachable and ultra-friendly Progressive spokesperson, has been living under a rock for the last ten years. She has appeared in well over 100 Progressive commercials since 2008.

And each of these commercials is fun-loving and silly. Unlike Allstate, who wants to be your caregiver, Progressive projects the style of wanting to be your buddy, someone you can trust and count on without taking things too seriously. Progressive's style has worked out great, as insurance is a heavy topic that nobody likes to deal with; therefore, providing a style that is lighthearted and upbeat can be seen as a reprieve.

Neither is right or wrong in its approach. Both insurance companies are doing just fine, even though their styles are very, very different. Progressive's manner of expression—how they go about showcasing to consumers their products and services—is different from Allstate's manner of expressing the *same* products and services.

So, there is no right or wrong way for you to generate a style in your soap and skin care business. But, you can't half-ass it. Progressive couldn't be silly and goofy *and* come off as being a caregiver. It wouldn't be sincere. It wouldn't be genuine. Whatever style path you create, you must go all in. Come original, and do so all the way.

CREATING CUSTOMERS WHO WANT TO BUY

In much the same way you formulate a product, adjust the recipe when needed, improve this and improve that, get rid of an unnecessary ingredient, add a necessary one, etc., you can do the same with formulating your customer.

Remember, you can't please everyone. You must hone in on a specific demographic, which is a specific segment of the population having shared characteristics. If one person in a certain demographic likes your products, there is a strong likelihood that other people in the same demographic will like your products. We will cover this in more detail in chapter seven.

BUD LIGHT & BUDWEISER

Let's look at two different, but incredibly strategic brands, Bud Light and Budweiser. Obviously, these two brands are owned by the same company, Anheuser Busch InBev, so it behooves them to effectively distinguish the two to maximize overall profits. It would be injudicious of them to advertise each beer in the exact same way. With that said, I want you to consider how these two brands differentiate themselves from each other in order to maximize profits. Furthermore, I want you to consider how your soap and skin care company can effectively pull in a specific demographic based on the messages you give. Be thinking of your company's customer base and how you engineer that base as you read the following:

For the last several decades, Bud Light has created an atmosphere of fun, playfulness, male-driven gags, and affordability. This has worked exceptionally well. Young people, still in the party scene, purchase Bud Light for merrymaking, get-togethers to watch the game, or have a barbecue. Bud Light has been Young America's go-to malted beverage for decades.

Bud Light *created* this customer base. They pulled in a certain demographic by succinctly and efficiently sending influential messages to them. If I was a hard-working, fun-loving young professional who was occasionally cash-strapped, Bud Light would be my beer, no question. And keep in mind that Bud Light didn't pull in this customer demographic based on taste. *Some of their commercials never even mention the taste of the product.*

Now let's consider Budweiser. Budweiser's branding and marketing efforts are very different from Bud Light's. Budweiser has a heavy focus on nostalgia, blue-collar pride and simple ingredients. Market research in recent years has painted a telling portrait of the typical Budweiser drinker. They are 42 percent more likely to drive a pick-up truck, and 68 percent more likely to use a credit card with flexible payment terms, which tells us that many of them don't have a lot of disposable income. Budweiser drinkers are typically middle-class and working-class, both of whom are stereotypically patriotic. Budweiser has branded itself as American as apple pie, including oversized pick-up trucks, American flag tattoos, and teary-eyed bald eagles.

Thus, while Bud Light's targeted audience has been focused on younger, fun-loving folks with an amusing sense of humor, Budweiser focused on patriotic, blue-collar folks in a slightly older demographic.

This was a very smart approach. By stretching two different (but *very* similar tasting) beer brands across two different demographics, Anheuser Busch InBev has cornered the macro beer world.

And here is the major takeaway from this targeted approach to defining a customer base…

THEY COULD HAVE BEEN SWITCHED

The decision for Bud Light to target the younger audience, while Budweiser the older demographic, was completely arbitrary. They could have switched demographics, issuing Budweiser as the fun-loving one, and Bud Light as the more majestic one.

In other words, there is no ingredient or brewing process in Budweiser that conjures up favorability in an older, more patriotic audience. Likewise, there is no ingredient or brewing process in Bud Light that attracts a younger, fun-loving audience. They *formulated* their customer base through a completely subjective branding and marketing application for each brand. Anheuser Busch InBev trained an entire country (and beyond) when, why and how to consume these two products, strictly based on the *perception* of each brand, not the *taste* of the actual product!

Take that in. Think about the implications of this with your company.

This is the beauty of branding and marketing. Through their overall visual appeal and marketing messages—*not the ingredients*—each beer brand manufactured a customer demographic that would be attracted to each respective brand. Again, this was not done through taste preference, but emotional perception. And this approach for both brands has worked brilliantly for over three decades.

BUT TIMES, THEY ARE CHANGING...

Much like artisan coffee, the craft beer industry has ballooned. Nowadays, it is becoming less and less cool or hip for the younger audience—mainly millennials—to drink Bud Light. Both men and women are switching to craft beers with an emphasis on their respective local producers. Furthermore, these craft beer consumers are spending more, because they care about how the beer is made and where the ingredients come from, which makes inexpensive, commodity beer seem "cheap."

Thus, Bud Light is making drastic changes to capture American millennials. They no longer want to be portrayed as the laughingstock of the beer industry, even though that has actually worked to their advantage since the early 1980s. They are no longer implementing the fun-loving, silly marketing messages that have worked for over 30 years, as they are no longer working.

Bud Light realizes that consumers are changing, society is changing, and there is an opportunity for their *brand* to change. To remain relevant in today's beer-purchasing world, they knew they needed a modification to how they were being perceived.

Unlike the original, timeless Budweiser can and bottle, the iconic "AB" crest-style logo has been absent from the Bud Light can and bottle for about 15 years. Not anymore. With the design revival of the archetypal logo, Bud Light has completely rebranded their cans and bottles to appear more ingredient-driven, with a harking back to the traditional messages of Anheuser-Busch. The product labels now appear more monotone, with shades of blue, a color that denotes trust.

Bud Light is trying to emphasize authenticity in its design, which is a brilliant move in the age of craft beer. With millennials' acute awareness of when and how they're being marketed to and the increased importance of authenticity, I believe we can expect to see more authenticity-driven branding from Anheuser-Busch InBev in the foreseeable future.

Oh, the power of perception!

DIET COKE & COCA-COLA ZERO

Let's look at another branding endeavor. While Diet Coke has been a leading sugar-free soft drink since it was first released in 1982, it came to light that young adult males shied away from this beverage, identifying diet cola as a woman's drink. The company's answer to that predicament came in 2005, in the form of a shiny black can, with the release of Coca-Cola Zero.

While Diet Coke was created with its own flavor profile and not as a sugar-free version of the original, Coca-Cola Zero aims to taste just like the "real Coke flavor." Despite their polar-opposite advertising campaigns, the contents and nutritional information of the two sugar-free colas is *nearly identical*. There *are* miniscule differences in the two products, so let's compare:

Diet Coke:

Nutritional Information: 0 Calories, 0g Fat, 40mg Sodium, 0g Total Carbs, 0g Protein.

Ingredients: Carbonated water, caramel color, aspartame, phosphoric acid, potassium benzonate, natural flavors, citric acid, caffeine.

Coca-Cola Zero:

Nutritional Information: 0 Calories, 0g Fat, 40mg Sodium, 0g Total Carbs, 0g Protein.

Ingredients: Carbonated water, caramel color, phosphoric acid, aspartame, potassium benzonate, natural flavors, potassium citrate, acesulfame potassium, caffeine.

As you can see, these two products are nearly identical.

THE VERDICT

The Huffington Post conducted a blind taste test between Diet Coke and Coca-Cola Zero, to which *only 54 percent of the tasters could distinguish Diet Coke from Coca-Cola Zero.*

Thus, it is a real toss-up in the actual difference (and/or preference) between the two products. Why? Because they are *virtually identical* in ingredients and taste. And, this was intentional on their part. They weren't trying to reinvent the wheel. They knew they had a solid product in Diet Coke, so why go to drastic measures to change it?

By essentially creating the same product, only branding one in a stark black can with red letters to counter the more feminine silver can, Coca-Cola was able to bring the male demographic into the fold in much larger numbers than they had seen before in one of their diet products. Young males are now essentially (though not technically) drinking diet coke without the stigma of it being a feminine product.

Think about the implications these examples can have with *your* business! The psychology behind these examples is extraordinary!

CUSTOMERS ARE FICKLE

The handcrafter must draw a line in the sand between constantly making product on one hand, and honing their company's branding appeal on the other. I'm more than positive that you make a great product. But not enough folks will buy your product if it doesn't look the part. Style matters.

Most of us in this industry find ourselves in love with the creative process of soapmaking and product formulation. We put all our emphasis into crafting. Our love of the process, combined with the uniqueness and utility of the products we make, create a drive in us big enough to start our very own business.

And many of us who start down this entrepreneurial path do not have any formal business background or education. What we *do* have is a passion for crafting premium products.

So, we make and make and make! But many of us don't sell and sell and sell...

What we fail to realize, because our passion is directed almost entirely on our products, is how fickle and unpredictable consumers are about appearances.

GENERALLY, AS HANDCRAFTERS...

...the emphasis is on what is *inside* the packaging (our product), therefore we don't really consider the actual *need* for quality packaging.

...the emphasis is on the incredible quality of our products; therefore, we don't really consider how our logo can be off-putting or incorrectly conveyed through poor design and lack of foresight.

...the emphasis is on elegant designs in our soap, therefore we assume that printing labels from our old dusty inkjet will suffice.

After all, once the customer gets over the inferior logo, irregular packaging, erratic overall design and cut-with-scissors label, they are going to love the actual product!

And, this is actually true!

For those wonderful customers who *do* overlook the inferior perception that our kitchen-crafted products showcase in comparison to more polished brands, they do fall in love with our products, because well, they're awesome!

Alas, there just aren't enough of these kind souls out there. Especially nowadays. You will, and probably have already, developed a recurrently-returning customer base that loves your products for what they provide, which is exceptional quality in all facets. They took a chance when others didn't, and it paid off for them *and* for you. But, these kind souls—often family and friends—are the exception to the cutthroat nature of consumerism rule. Furthermore, there just aren't enough of these buyers around for you to put *real* money in your pocket. People want to be moved emotionally before they purchase, especially if the product is set at a higher price point than they are accustomed. They want excitement. They want depth. They want a story. They need aesthetics in all aspects – company name, logo, mission, storyline, background, color schemes, fonts, packaging, beautifully designed websites, enticing pictures on Instagram, etc.

NEEDS & WANTS

There are two types of purchases made by all consumers; needs and wants. Mega-retailers like Wal-Mart and Target emphasize their retail supply chain on needs (there are of course "wants" in their stores, but you get the gist). You, as a handcrafted soap and skincare business owner, must create a "want" in the minds and hearts of potential buyers.

WHY A WANT AND NOT A NEED?

Soap has always been a commodity-driven product to be found and sold all over the world at relatively low prices; thus, *no one needs your soap.* They can go purchase a half dozen Dove or Ivory bars for the price of only one of your bars. Ever heard that one? But, there are plenty of folks out there who *want* your soap, right?

But why do they want it? And who are they?

VOICE MATTERS

If you were to ask a 20-year old woman from rural, Appalachian Kentucky to read a sentence from a book, and then asked a 20-year old woman from Queens, New York to read the same sentence, they would sound completely different, and I'm not just talking about their accent. The demeanor, flow, cadence and overall style of each would sound so different that it might be difficult to determine the same sentence was even being read. Their overall voice, the original expression they use, ultimately determines how the sentence will come across to others. *Their tone and projection actually shapes the way we receive the message.*

One of the biggest mistakes newfound soap and skincare companies make is not paying enough attention to their company's tone of voice. Worse, perhaps, is that many companies *don't even have a voice.*

Yes, companies should spend a great deal of time on logos, color selection and other efforts towards a solid brand, but only *after* they take the time to consider the benefits of employing a unique voice. If you were to mask the logo on your website, would your company *sound* unique? Or would you sound like everyone else? Remember, it isn't *what* you say but *how* you say it. Developed correctly, your tone of voice can be the secret sauce in your company's content formula.

THE 'PERSONA' OF YOUR BUSINESS

Imagine your budding soap and skincare company as if it were a person in real life. Every aspect of your business has come to life, forming the ideal, personified version of your company. Who does this "person" resonate with the most? Who do they hang out with? Where do they spend most of their free time?

A company's persona and style has to have resonance with customers and prospects for it to work. It has to not only vibrate with your own ultimate vision, but most importantly, it must resonate with your audience. If your personified company were to hang out with their most ideal friends, what kind of people would they be? Chances are, these friends are the type who will ultimately become your customers.

Would your personified company hang out with the likes of Oprah? Or maybe a Marine veteran? Or perhaps a busy Mother of three? These are all extreme examples, which I have done on purpose to showcase a simple point – you must know who you are resonating with, because style is selective.

Some companies take this approach very literally. Betty Crocker, for example, was a fictional, prototypical persona that became one of the most recognized faces in America. Other examples that *literally* anthropomorphize their company's style are Aunt Jemima, Uncle Ben and the Pillsbury Dough Boy. These of course, are all invented, cartoonish characters. Some companies use personification *even more literally*, such as Mary Kay, Paul Mitchell, Donald Trump, Coco Chanel, Norton AntiVirus, etc. The style of the company is completely enthralled with what these personas—both real and fictional—attempt to represent. Whether or not you actualize the use of a persona (real or fictional), your company should still have its own identity, equipped with its own style.

PERSONIFYING YOUR COMPANY:

Who is my company?

...Is it similar to a person? If so, is it male or female? Both? Or, is it an animal? If so, what kind of animal? Is it fictitious (unicorn) or real (horse)? What is the makeup of my company?

What does my company represent?

...Honesty? Intelligence? Humor? Beauty? Courage? Daring? Feminism? Honor? Comedy? Rock n' Roll? Punk? Rural life? Global outreach? America first? Sports? Family? Animals? Nature? Travel? Urban life? Fun? Fashion?

What is my company's appearance?

...Buttoned up? Bohemian? Hipster? Laid back? Jeans & Tee Shirt? Victoria Secret? L.L. Bean? Young? Timeworn? Nerdy? Urban? Sophisticated? Country? Metro? Naked? Chic?

What is my company's disposition?

Fun-loving? Serious? Care-free? Militant? Sophisticated? Care-giving? Hilarious? Laid-back? Zany? Salt-of-the-Earth?

Just for fun, let's look at the above questions and Frankenstein our way into a character personification for a business. The first question asks who my company is. After thinking it through, I surmise that my company lends itself to taking on the personification of a young woman. In my mind's eye, I see her in her 30s. She is taking on more and more responsibility at work, but still holds on to her rebel youth. Her wardrobe is unusual, seeking out old, dusty rags from vintage clothing stores that she pairs with $200 shoes, which she pulls off well, as she is complimented often.

She carries the latest iPhone, and she often uses it to shop online. She is definitely buttoned-down after work, but more stoic and representative while clocked-in. She earns $50,000 a year.

Even though she lives in the big city, she and her friends, male and female, will often take weekend trips into regional, state and national parks to camp, drink wine and eat s'mores. They take day hikes around the area while camping. If anyone was daring enough to skinny dip in a cold stream, it was her. She is care-free and takes fun seriously. She is silly and has a magnetic personality. She works hard and plays hard.

She buys her groceries at health food stores and from local producers at weekend farmer's markets. She cares about good ingredients, but isn't pugnacious about them. She likes what she likes, and is easily marketed to. The idea of natural products appeals to her, but she also uses other skin care and household products that don't necessarily represent a natural product. She loves the newest look in design, style and fashion, which is clean, industrial and minimal. Softer, chic color palettes appeal to her, and these color combinations are represented in her downtown apartment.

Her name is Lily.

From this description, which I completely made up while writing this at 5:15 in the morning, we can now see how to market our style, voice and overall aesthetics to best represent my newfound company persona, Lily.

Let's say we keep delving into this persona, develop a company name, mission and a unique voice:

"At Chic Soapworks, we believe that a fun, modern lifestyle is about being, not having. Things we do shape who we are, the lifestyle we lead and the choices we make. Chic Soapworks is about having unique life experiences that are connected by the ever-important commitment to skin and body nourishment.

As a society, we are moving from opulent to meaningful, from possessive to experiential. Today's woman is interlinked with identity, self-expression and lifestyle. We know you want newness and a sense of discovery in all facets of life, including skin and body nourishment.

We believe in the power of passion, creativity and unique materials that make up our product line. Discover Chic Soapworks."

Again, this was all made up on the fly, it now being 5:40 a.m.

Whether you actually like my made-up concept above is not the point. The point is that I took the time to close my eyes and visualize the persona of a company for the writing of this book. I literally saw Lily, this young woman, in my mind's eye. I saw her interests, hobbies and proclivities. Then I wrote it down. Then I created a company name, style, voice and message from Lily.

From this, I can already see in my mind's eye the chic, boutique style design of the website. I can see the fonts being used. I can see the simple color palette across all marketing materials. I can see a simple yet elegant logo.

You see I could, if I truly wanted, *actually* create this company with an incredible and unique style, obtain a domain name and start selling as soon as my products were ready in the next month or two. Moreover, I know that I would immediately be more successful than most startups in our industry. No, I'm not bragging. Trust me, I have no ego-investment in me writing these words. I say this to illustrate to you the dire need for style and voice, and the utter lack of it I see in most companies in our industry.

Furthermore, as of this writing, I am a 35-year old bald dude from Missouri. I am clearly not the company persona, nor am I my targeted customer in this example. I am not even close to being Lily!

And guess what? That is perfectly fine! Who says *you* have to be like your customer? Who says *you* have to take on the persona of your business?

I took the time to close my eyes and visualize a person into being, someone completely made up. Maybe my subconscious comprised images of different people I've known over the years, or even just passed by on the street once. Maybe in a previous life I was a hip, 30-something female who liked to skinny-dip. Who knows, but the point is that I just ran with it once I closed my eyes and started typing. Lily anchored the entirety of my company's aesthetic position in the marketplace.

Who is your Lily?

VALUE PERCEPTION

If we lived in a world where the value of a good was indisputably equal to its price tag, branding would not exist. Thankfully for entrepreneurs, we live in a world where people come up with their *own* interpretation of the perceived value of a good. We can use market value perception to our advantage as handcrafters if only we put in our due diligence.

If a customer's perceived value is *greater* than the price tag, in most circumstances they will buy. If it is not, they won't. It's as simple as that.

And think about it; if they've never purchased from your company before, the only thing they have to go on is the smell (if applicable), the feel, the name, logo, packaging design and overall aesthetic. And that is only in a "physical" scenario. If on your website, a perusing potential online customer must be wowed into seeing and feeling immense value through:

→ The overall look and feel of your website.

→ The quality and precision of your product photography.

→ The attention to detail regarding the descriptions of each product.

→ The names of each product.

→ The name of your company.

→ The logo of your company, and where it is placed on your site.

→ The messages you are providing.

This is how a potential customer will assess your product's value, not by the smell and touch, but through an emotional tug that *you* create. Thus, it becomes obvious to spend more and more time, money and resources on these aspects of your business moving forward, as opposed to focusing too heavily on crafting.

PRODUCT PACKAGING

Most customers don't have the time or energy to weigh the advantages and disadvantages of the products they are looking at, whether in person or online, so they use a shortcut to make their decision. That shortcut is your product's packaging and photography. Does this make customers a bit fickle? Yes! But that is the business world we live in!

Packaging is one of the single most powerful weapons you have in your branding arsenal because it tells consumers why your products and brand are different. And, it isn't just the packaging that is torn off or ripped open and eventually thrown away that is important. Plenty of savvy, artisan startups are mastering the unboxing experience as well. Online customers who shop for higher-end products have come to expect a beautiful unboxing occasion, and you must follow suit to keep up.

HOW CAN YOU MAKE YOUR PACKAGING STAND OUT?

First of all, know your demographic. For example, what colors would entice your specific niche market? The colors used in your product packaging play a key role in consumer buying decisions. Our brains react to colors in different ways, so choose your packaging colors accordingly. For example, products with white packaging convey simplicity, safety and purity. Color experts cite that the more color added to a product's package, the less sophisticated the product appears, but this isn't necessarily the case in all industries. Other colors, like blue, convey many different meanings. A light sky-blue color is considered more playful, while a dark navy is considered much more trusting and professional. Worldwide, blue is the most liked color, but that doesn't mean you should automatically choose it. It's important to study your target demographic before deciding on a color scheme for your product packaging. Be bold and creative in how you approach product packaging and think about *who* is going to like it.

Similarly, when taking into consideration *who* you are targeting, recyclable or reusable packaging is always a reason for a certain demographic to choose your brand over a competitor. In fact, 52 percent of people around the world make purchase decisions partially due to packaging that shows a brand making a positive social and environmental impact. A decision such as this really comes down to who you are trying to target with your products and packaging, along with how this might fall in line (or out of line) with your company's mission.

Ultimately, your product's packaging is meant to communicate a purpose – what your brand stands for and what it means for your customer. Don't miss this opportunity to create a lasting impression on the shelf (or website) and in the minds of your customers.

PRODUCT PHOTOGRAPHY

If you are selling or plan to sell online, please place utmost importance in your product's photography. Photography is crucial when it comes to selling your soap and skin care products online. Whether it is soap or a leave-on product, the two primary sensations that people value most with your products are smell and touch, *neither of which they will be able to engage in when shopping on your site*. If you have inferior product pictures in *our industry*, people will be profoundly less receptive to making a purchase. But, if your product shots are outstanding, customers will *immediately* notice and will be profoundly more willing to add to cart. Using photography well is what will ultimately sell your product, period.

Unless you are simply awesome at photography and have a great camera, I would at least look around for some good photographers to take your shots for you. Whether you take them yourself or hire out, keep in mind some of these simple product-photography ideals:

- → Do not underestimate the value of simplicity. We want things to look and feel fluid, sleek, and minimal. A strong, clean photographic style creates a statement that is bigger than just one product. Stripping out the clutter in your imagery and focusing on the product not only creates a more versatile image that you can use for multiple things, but can also help elevate the perceived value of your products, and your brand as a whole. This of course should only be followed *if it fits your brand.*
- → Do not forget the context of the image and the background. Whether you want a stark-white background to promote a clean and minimal look or place your products on old woodgrain, the key here is the age-old mantra – be consistent, and make sure the background *fits your brand.*
- → Consider the design of your website, when preparing photo shoots (always think "cohesion"). Will the design work best with landscape, portrait or square images? Is there enough space or contrast to allow for text to be used alongside or on top of the image? In an ideal world, the web-designer (whether it be you or someone else) should be given a *library* of quality images at the start to enable you (or them) to shape the design around it, resulting in a far better design process.
- → Consider alternative views of each product – close-ups, above, from the side, etc. The more detailed options you can then present to your potential customer, the more they understand the value of the product with fewer questions.

→ Use high-resolution photography as much as possible. Not only does this showcase the product best, it also allows for clearer images on retina screens (phones, tablets, etc.) and the ability to add a detailed zoom feature to the website.

We, the business owner, get to shake things up with colorful emotions, beautiful backstories and crystal-clear visions. Then we can manufacture a completed "image" of a beautiful company in all facets to cater to the people we know are willing to purchase. This is the power of perceived value.

There is a psychology behind *selling* a good product, which goes far beyond *making* a good product. Thousands and thousands of start-up businesses must close their doors too soon – not because of the lack of quality in their products, but because of their lack of a strong, foundational message.

I compare soapmakers to nurses or teachers, in that we are care givers. I truly believe that. In creating, through chemistry, an invaluable product that provides the user with both cleanliness and a genuine, intimate experience, you are providing great care. So, my message to you is not to run from it. Take pride and ownership of what you do, and showcase that to your customers.

You get to create your ideal customer. And your ideal customer will have friends. You can provide care for all of them. You *get* to do this through your business. If you are afraid of outright sales and marketing, it might help to think of what you are doing in a different way. Pivot your mind away from sales tactics and wishful purchases into being a care giver. This mental switch will aid you in branding your company to a very specific demographic, and they will reciprocate your care-giving approach with purchases. And over time, these purchases can provide you with a truly wonderful life.

Having money is the byproduct of people, circumstances and events. As the owner of your business, you get to shape the people, circumstances and events in order to receive money. Don't be afraid of this power. Harness it.

Nothing in life worth pursuing is going to be easy. We now live in a world of instant gratification, and sometimes we take this approach internally, meaning that if we don't knock something out of the park on the first try, we might tell ourselves that it isn't worth pursuing. *You must practice stick-to-it-iveness.*

HAVE FUN!

And most of all, this should be fun. If it isn't fun, you probably aren't doing it right. You get to creatively invent a company with its own persona and character. You get to dream on behalf of your business, and then share that dream with others. You get to create a beautiful color palette, search for the perfect fonts, conjure up the perfect names for your products with inventive descriptions. You *get* to do this!

CHAPTER 6:

WHAT'S IN A NAME?

"Young fella, if you're looking for trouble, I'll accommodate Ya."

If you're of a certain age, or just a fan, you know this famous movie quote came from the 1969 film, *True Grit*, the stark line emitted with perfect timing and mastery from America's most iconic actor in the western film genre, Marion Mitchell Morrison.

Wait, Who?...

Otherwise known as John Wayne.

WHAT'S IN A NAME?

A lot, when it comes to your company's success. The right name can make your company the talk of the town. The wrong one can doom it to obscurity and failure. Ideally, your company's name should convey the value and uniqueness of the products you have developed while striking a tone of intrigue and excitement.

Some experts believe that the best names are abstract, a blank slate upon which to create an image (Pinterest). Others think that names should be informative so customers know immediately what your business is (Best Buy). Some believe that coined names, that come from made-up words, are more memorable than names that use real words (Google). Others think they're silly.

The truth is, any name can be effective as long as it's backed by the appropriate mission and strategy. Naming your company is the first step towards building a solid brand with a strong, foundational message. You must really think it through, and as always, consider thinking bigger.

PARALLEL, NOT PERPENDICULAR

It goes without saying that the name of your company should run parallel to the foundational elements that make up your business, but there are many, inside and outside of our industry, that fail to make this discernable connection.

If your business is driven towards luxury, extravagance and sumptuousness, then you probably don't want to name it, "Earl's Super Good Soaps n' Such." Is your business driven towards natural beauty with simple, minimal concepts and tones? Then you probably don't want to name it, "Opulent Indulgence."

YOUR NAME, YOUR CUSTOMER

Who is your customer? This question will be examined deeper in the following chapter, but the subject should be broached here, as the name of your company will very much determine whose interest you are peaking. We tend to want to be all things to all people, but truly successful products-based businesses just don't work that way. You must know who your perfect and ideal customer is and market directly to them, and that starts with the name.

- → If you want to name your company "Sugar Mama's Skin Care," you probably aren't going to get a lot of male consumers, even if you offer men's grooming products. If you are okay with this, no worries. But, if you want to produce products that are more gender-neutral based on who you want your customer to be, you might want to reconsider the name.

- → If you want to name your company "Gulf Coast Soaps," you probably aren't going to get a lot of first-time purchasers from California or Oregon, even with an effective online marketing program. My own business, Prairie Soap Company, ran into this problem when trying to sell to a store in Maine. I never thought it would be an issue because I wasn't thinking big enough. I'm not saying you can't get customers from elsewhere, but you would obviously be pigeon-holing your company's base to a certain location. This type of naming is usually done in a very well-traveled environment, often touristy, to serve as a destination for those who live outside of the general location.

→ If you are deeply religious and want to name your company accordingly, you might immediately eliminate any potential consumer who is agnostic, atheist or simply on the fence about their personal beliefs. If you are okay with this, no worries. But like it or not, agnostics and atheists are both increasing in numbers in the United States, and they also need soap.

LOOK FROM ALL SIDES

It is easy to get caught up in naming your company after some vestige of you, whether it is where you live, your personal beliefs, your name, the street where you grew up, the nickname your spouse gave your firstborn, etc. Of course, there is nothing wrong with this, but make sure to think bigger if in fact you want to grow your business dealings outside of your own personal, intimate circle of family and society.

What about approaching your company name from your potential customer's perspective? What would *they* admire, be intrigued by and appreciate from a name? If, for example, based on your mission, vision, values and product offerings, you know your primary customer base is going to be women, ages 18-65 with disposable income, who shop at Whole Foods, drive SUVs and don't mind spending a bit extra on a quality Chardonnay. Which name would better fit? "Luxe Essentials" or "Lathers by Frank." I'm not suggesting there is an obvious best answer, as this truly is a subjective undertaking. But, being as objective as possible, can you see how "Lathers by Frank" can be slightly less appealing to the targeted demographic versus "Luxe Essentials?" You don't come first. Your customers do. At least consider naming your company in a way that reflects the behavior and inclinations that your targeted customer base has.

Let's look at how a successful name reflects the customer base:

LUSH

Lush a truly amazing company name. Removing your own industry-specific sensibilities and being as objective as possible, you can see how the name, "Lush" plays well to their specific, targeted consumer base, primarily well-to-do, suburban women and teeny-boppers who have cash to spend.

APPLE

Whether you are a die-hard mac person or prefer a PC, you can't deny such a friendly name as Apple, especially when compared to Microsoft, which certainly sounds more corporate/techy. Apple is an inviting, approachable name that attracts A LOT of people. Specific values and beliefs are attached to the name, and their brand is solidified because of it. You think of more than their products; you think of Steve Jobs, elegant design, fun commercials and the like. I am Apple's targeted customer, and I see how they have funneled me into preferring them over others, and it started with the name.

NIKE

Ever heard of them? The shoe company, turned all things clothing and sports gear, embraces the spirit of victory, thus consulting Greek mythology to find their muse – Nike, the Winged Goddess of Victory. Since they've been around forever and are such a massive company, it is easy to forget how truly amazing the name is. Seemingly every athlete, want-to-be athlete and weekend gym warrior in the world wears Nike.

JUNIPER RIDGE

My all-time favorite company in the world of soap and skin care, the name Juniper Ridge sounds intriguing, mysterious, natural and completely gender neutral. They nailed their name, as I personally conceptualize Juniper Ridge as being intriguing, mysterious, natural and completely gender neutral. And, if I do say so myself, I believe this to be a spot-on analysis, as I am their perfect and ideal customer.

HÄAGEN-DAZS

In my opinion, this is one of the coolest brand names ever. Why? Because the name doesn't actually mean anything. Even still, the name Häagen-Dazs is synonymous with the product it sells. That is hard to do.

THE IMPERIAL DRIFTER (AND MY NAMING PROCESS)

The Imperial Drifter is a progressive men's grooming company I named (I have since sold the business) with a unique, foundational message within the larger marketplace of men's grooming. Because of the women's empowerment background and all the travel required of me for our non-profit, I thought it would be distinctive to incorporate a strong sense of wander *(and "wonder")* and equality with the brand. That was our hook. Wanderlust meets manly-chic meets empowerment.

Though the Imperial Drifter is not me, I used myself, and who I strive to be, as the brand's persona or avatar. Here was the process:

WRITE!

Yes, I know – how surprising of me to explain how I used the written word and will subsequently recommend you do the same!

As the brand's wanna-be avatar, the first thing I did was write out all of the things I love to do, be and have:

- → Hiking and backpacking
- → Traveling overseas—even to sketchy places
- → Road tripping in the U.S., camping in national parks, roughing it
- → Drinking craft beer and artisanal, small batch spirits
- → Living in an urban atmosphere (city life)
- → Caring about nature, the environment
- → Shopping at stores like L.L. Bean and REI, even if they are expensive!
- → Having nice things, not shopping at discount stores, only going to quality restaurants, etc.
- → Women's empowerment and social equality

After taking some time to write this short list of my favorite things to be, do and have, I noticed an obvious dichotomy in my list. On one hand, I love to backpack for days at a time without showering. I love to strike out on the road and discover where to lay my head at night without much planning. I love to travel overseas, even to the developing world, often eating sketchy food and lodging in strange places.

On the other hand, I very much like the finer things in life. I love to try new, fancy restaurants, even if it costs 50 dollars a plate. I thoroughly enjoy craft beer and artisanal spirits, and will pay a premium for them. I don't mind spending a bit more on the name brand clothes and shoes that suit me. I grew up eating cornbread, black-eyed peas and buttermilk often. I didn't enjoy the "finer things" in life, as my family did not have disposable income. So now, after working hard for what I've earned, I very much enjoy quality offerings, both in purchasing and in experience.

At first, I was distraught about the obvious clashing in my taste for things and zeal for life. How would this help me create a company name?

Then I asked myself, *"Could polar opposite enjoyments of life conceptually work in a business name?*

I went on to tackle naming my company from a different perspective, namely the ingredients used and how they might conjure up a certain set of emotions:

- → Essential oils
    - → Woodsy, earthy, spicy
- → No preservatives or synthetics
- → Pure, plant-derived oils and butters from around the world
    - → Unrefined shea butter from Ghana
    - → Beeswax from bees
    - → Argan oil from northern Africa

- → Feelings of nature, using natural products
- → Feelings of expansiveness in terms of the harvesting of raw materials
- → High quality, Earth-driven, etc.

So, now I had a rough list of ingredients and how they might make customers feel, as well as my company avatar's list of things he loves to be, do and have. After looking over my lists, I decided to better visualize the process with a diagram.

On poster board, I drew three huge circles, all of which intersected each other in the middle of the three circles. In geometry terminology, I believe I constructed a "union" of three circles.

- → In the first circle was the first list of things I like to be, do and have as it relates to wander, travel and roughing it.
- → The second circle was the list of things I like to be, do and have as it relates to the finer things in life.
- → The third circle was the list of ingredients and the emotions that might be invoked by them.

So, there it was, staring me in the face. I knew the name of my company was in the union of those three circles. How could I tie these three concepts into one idea, one name? After scribbling away on a list of contradictory-cum-complimentary phrases with the use of a handy thesaurus, I came up with THE IMPERIAL DRIFTER.

The word, "drifter" exemplifies my lust for travel and exploration, whether it be abroad or right here in the United States. The word, "imperial" exemplifies a royal and refined taste for the assortment that life has to offer. Either word by themselves would not fit into the brand. Thus, The Imperial Drifter is the ever-present *balance* between two opposites, which is what many men wrestle with on a daily basis. I often think of an Imperial Drifter as someone who lives and works in New York City, enjoys all of his urban proximities, yet drives into the mountains and backcountries upstate to experience nature and establish a balance between two worlds. This exemplifies what it means to be an Imperial Drifter.

With a strong foundational message already established, I now had the perfect name. The Imperial Drifter name—along with its mission, vision and values—laid the groundwork for all other branding components, such as product packaging, fonts, the logo, arrangements of color on any given piece of marketing material, the look and feel of the website, etc.

Put simply, I would not have been able to accelerate the success of the company without giving my all to the budding idea I knew was inside me. It took several days to conjure up a vision, a strong mission, overall message and name, but it was all worth the effort of inner-exploration and creativity. You certainly don't have to use my method above to name your company. I encourage you to think broadly and creatively in any way that suits you.

FIRST IMPRESSIONS

Entire relationships are dictated by first impressions, so making a powerful impact immediately is a necessary key to the branding success. The first thing a customer interacts with is a name, so it has to convey the right message; it has to wow your audience. Think of it as a first handshake; it says a lot about the person and makes a powerful impression. A great name has the power to build a long-lasting relationship between a company and customers, but it has the power to ruin otherwise great potential relationships.

DUCKS AND EAGLES

Ducks tend to stick together, comprising a flock. Eagles are autonomous and self-directed. Ducks quack back and forth, waddling in their own mess. Eagles soar above the untidiness, sending its unique and discernible call to express itself. Eagles have profound eyesight, piercing past needlessness to locate its' specific target.

Are you a duck or an eagle?

I believe unequivocally that there is enough room for all in this industry to be successful. I firmly believe this; however, there is enough room for success *only* if everyone thinks and acts like an eagle. You can't be successful in this industry by thinking and acting like a duck.

Slopping together a name for your company without foresight and planning is being a duck. Your company will be muddled and confused, waddling around in fruitless revenue streams. If you want to provide for yourself and your family by starting and running a company, come up with a good name for it. Be autonomous like an eagle. Soar above what everyone else is doing and think outside the box. Search outside of our immediate industry for inspiration. Find a muse if you must (the Goddess, Nike) and dedicate your company to its aura. Perhaps you could create an avatar—a character—that upholds all the values your company will showcase to the world.

Everything matters. Everything is connected. It takes milliseconds for people to find inauthenticity in a business, and it starts with the name.

LIVE UP TO YOUR NAME

Every component of your business must follow the company's name. As previously discussed, if your brand is to be focused on exceptionalism and luxury, the name must exemplify this. Furthermore, your company must then come up with a "voice" that matches the name, denoting exceptionalism and luxury (see previous chapter). Or, if you want your company to be funny and lighthearted, make sure your name complements this, and then brand all other business components accordingly.

If you recall my made-up company, "Earth & Salt Soapworks," there was an obvious dedication to it being an earthy and natural business. Consider, for example, how a company such as this would create their product descriptions. They probably wouldn't want to use words like, "yummy" or "scrumptious" or "bubbly-goodness." These words don't represent the name of the company or its intentions. Everything has to be thought through, and it all begins with the name. You must go all in for your customers to go all in. If you think your company is slopped together, so too will your customers.

BUSINESS NAME & DOMAIN NAME

For your business to thrive, you need a unique website. Let's just get that out of the way right now. And, there is an incredibly strong argument for checking a certain URL's availability before deciding wholeheartedly on a company name. Let's say you come up with the perfect business name, obtain an EIN number and start a business, only to discover that the domain name is already taken by some company in south Florida that markets and sells adult diapers.

This reason alone—not being able to obtain the correct domain for your company name—might be a strong enough reason to think of another company name altogether (according to some). A company name with a non-matching domain name may spell disaster for your business, especially if a strong online revenue stream is your foremost intention.

Ten years ago, it was pretty easy to get a domain that matched your company. Now, not so much. The internet is flooded with new websites every single day. Nowadays, you'd be really lucky if the dot-com URL that matches your new business name is readily available, *unless of course you generate a highly unique and creative name*. The more generic and "universal" your company name is, the harder it will be to guarantee the URL (A Uniform Resource Locator, colloquially termed a web address).

So, what do you do? What has priority? Do you pick a company name based on whether there's an exact-match domain name available? Or do you get creative with the URL to fit the business name of your dreams?

In my estimation, you first need to decide *how* you are going to make your money:

STRONG ONLINE REVENUE STREAM:

If your business model revolves around the Web, or if you're planning to spend a lot of money on online marketing, then an exact-match domain name should be a top priority. I know you probably don't consider yourself on the same level as Netflix, Yelp, Spotify or even Google, but hear me out...When someone says Google, everyone knows what they are talking about. Nobody says, "Google Dot Com." Why would you say, "dot com?" Everyone understands that it is a website. You see, *the word has become synonymous with its function and purpose.* Likewise, nobody says, "Netflix Dot Com" You see, the name *is* the website. If you really think about it, that is an impressive thing to accomplish as an online business.

If you delve wholeheartedly into online retail, you will want people to eventually default to your company name as your URL. This is a good thing! It means you are doing it right! But, if that URL directs them to someone else's site, you're obviously losing out on valuable business prospects.

We got lucky. My Mother had the foresight to obtain the domain name www.prairiesoapcompany.com in the late 90s, literally a decade before we ever actually built our website. Later, during the height of our business, we received emails and phone calls on a very regular basis from customers asking for something they loved, but it wasn't on our website. I would ask them what the product was, and they would tell me. I would then have to tell them that unfortunately, the product must be from a company with a similar name. I felt so terrible for the other companies (there are *a lot* of renditions of Prairie Soap Company out there), that I would actually track down the product and the right company and refer the mistaken customer to their desired shopping page. These other companies, all with very similar names to ours, didn't have the URL that was the easiest and shortest to remember. We did.

STRONG WHOLESALE (B2B) REVENUE STREAM:

If your customers are everyday online consumers, an exact-match URL is more important than if you're in the wholesale business, or business-to-business industry. B2B companies tend to sell to niche markets that have a smaller assortment of product lines (small assortment, large orders), generally making their pool of customers smaller than a retail setting. It isn't vital to have the exact domain in these scenarios.

STRONG OFFLINE REVENUE STREAM:

If the majority of your business is done offline, there's more flexibility if an exact-match domain name is not available. Many brick-and-mortar businesses, like restaurants, include their geographic location in their URLs. For example, think about companynameNY.com if you're in New York, or companynameSF.com if you're in San Francisco. This also will help increase your search engine visibility because many people search for retail outlets, eateries, hotels, etc. by location. They would do the same for your brick and mortar store.

THESE AREN'T THE RULES. *THERE ARE NO RULES.*

Everything mentioned above can be met with a stipulation to its validity. There are no hard and fast rules that dictate how you should go about naming your company with your domain name.

For a long while, Tesla didn't own the domain name Tesla.com. The difference, however, between your company and Tesla, is that they are a global company with a marketing and advertising budget that seemingly exceeds conception. Basically, they have formed a presence in our collective minds, so we don't *need* to know their domain name in order to find them. And for that reason, they didn't *have* to have Tesla.com. Do you think someone wanting to buy a Tesla gives up if they go there and don't find the website? Of course not! They type "Tesla cars" into a search engine and find it in no time flat. They probably wouldn't have even looked at the domain name, which by the way was TeslaMotors.com (they now own both). If Tesla doesn't have to have an exact match domain name, neither do you. But, keep in mind their presence compared to yours.

DOMAIN NAME EXTENSIONS

A domain extension is the notation at the end of a web address that specifies an Internet category or a country code. You are probably most familiar with .COM, but I'm sure you've seen .NET, .BIZ, .EDU and .ORG.

The correct extension plays a vital role in obtaining the perfect web address. If you've come up with the perfect name only to find that the .COM extension is unavailable, but the .NET or .BIZ *is* available, then you have a tough decision to make. .COM is obviously king, but you might be able to get away with a different extension as long as you market it very clearly. That said, some people will inevitably still never find you because the habitual pattern of typing, ".com" is very much ingrained in us.

SOCIAL MEDIA HANDLES

Make sure to check whether social media handles that match your new company are available. Ideally, they should all be the same as your domain name. If something's already taken, a small change to your brand name or adding an industry or location-specific modifier that's consistent across all your social media networks might be the way to go.

For example, if your domain name is happyhempsoap.com, but @happyhempsoap has already been taken on Twitter, consider @happyhempsoapco or @happyhempsoapKC (for Kansas City). This may not be the absolute ideal scenario, but you must work with what is available and make it consistent across all platforms.

TRADEMARK SEARCH

One of the worst things that can happen to a new business occurs when the owners spend time and money promoting a certain name, only to find out someone else has been using it. Even if they haven't registered a trademark, someone might own the rights simply because they were using it first. A quick Google search is an absolute must and you may want to supplement it with a professional trademark search.

STRATEGY MEETS CREATIVITY

As you can see, choosing a name for your new business should be a strategic decision, not purely based on creative inspiration. You must have a plan that goes beyond the upcoming week, or year or even three years. This is your life we are talking about! Naming your business needs to be a looked at from a distance, not just now. If you want to have a business that puts money in your pocket, it is time to start thinking bigger.

What if Amazon had been named Bookstore.com? They would be limited to selling books. They thought bigger and took a long-term approach. The Amazon we know today is not the same Amazon as when they launched. They had a strategy to get where they are, and that strategy included a name that wouldn't bottleneck their success in any way whatsoever. Conversely, Burlington Coat Factory is a prime example of how not to name a company. When they were naming their store, they didn't think far enough into the future. When they expanded their product offering, they had to change their tagline to, "We're more than just coats."

Bottom line, the origin of your company name should be an adventure. It should be vested in originality, kept simple for your customers and be the roots to your ever-growing company tree.

An oak tree has unique roots, a unique trunk and unique branches and leaves. An oak tree doesn't have chestnut leaves and a maple trunk. Every aspect of its being makes it an oak tree. If the name of your company is the root system, everything in your company must be cohesive and unique to its name. If the name (root system) of your company is to be fun and lighthearted, then your company's voice (the leaves) must also be fun and lighthearted, and so on.

Your company's name and all that follows must grow in planned-for unity and matchlessness.

PRODUCT NAMES & DESCRIPTIONS

These days, not just any name will do. In our flooded artisan industry, there are too many of the same names. Yes, you should certainly cater to a descriptive name that will authorize the product's utility and aid in its sale, but you should also think creatively about your approach. Your product name needs to fit within your broader brand name umbrella while telling its own unique story to consumers. It needs to be memorable, findable (particularly on search engines), unusual, understandable, and relevant. Let's look at how naming products can shape your business:

YOU COULD MAKE UP A WORD

The first place most business owners start when they have to name a product is to simply create a name that describes what the product does. With soap, that is easy – it's called "soap." But the descriptions *beyond* the utility of the word "soap" is what will make the sale. Indigo Wild, a truly fantastic soap and skin care company, came up with "Zum Bars" as the name of all their soaps. On each bar label, they have in big words, "Zum Bar," and underneath the name of the particular fragrance. Why "Zum?" On the very first line of many bullet-pointed, *did-you-knows* on their about page, Indigo Wild explains, *"Did you know 'Zum' is a made-up word?"*

So, there you go. They literally made up a word and dedicated it to the lion's share of their product line, bar soap. Indigo Wild (a very large artisan company who happens to be in the same city as myself and my old business) is synonymous with the word, "Zum." People would often come in my store, look around and then say something like, "Wow this is just like Zum!"

YOU COULD ADD A PREFIX OR SUFFIX

You don't have to make up a word for your actual commodity (soap, or anything else), but I give you this example to offer the idea that thinking outlandishly and funky can pay off in your branding schemes. Apple takes the same approach, as seemingly everything they manufacture has the wildly prevalent prefix, "i" in front of the product (iPhone, iPad, iPod). What does an "i" have to do with Apple? Inherently, nothing. But they identified all of their products this way and now they are synonymous with the brand. Brilliant.

YOU COULD USE THE POWER OF SUGGESTION

Words don't have to be used literally in product. Rather, they can be suggestive like The Imperial Drifter's "Trailhead" beard oil, which proposes an outdoorsy, woodsy scent combination. A customer has no idea the scent combination, but if he or she enjoys the outdoors or woodsy scents, the name will raise an eyebrow. I could have just named the product based on the scent combination. That would have been perfectly fine, but I decided to create intrigue by being suggestive.

YOU COULD MISSPELL ON PURPOSE

Something I've always wanted to try in a brand is misspelling names of products or descriptions on purpose. Products like Trix, Kix, Fantastik, and Liquid-Plumr use real words that are misspelled. It's creative and helps when the name you want is already trademarked or the related domain names are already taken.

YOU COULD USE COMPOUND WORDING

Since so many brand and product names are already trademarked and the associated domain names have already been registered, it's very common these days for product names to be compound words made by putting two words together to form an entirely new brand or product name. Think "Photoshop."

For example, a soap and skin care company could name their soaps with "bar" at the end of each, closing the compound:

- → "LavBar" for Lavender
- → "CharBar" for Charcoal
- → "TreeBar" for Tea Tree
- → "LemBar" for Lemon
- → "ChamBar" for Chamomile
- → "SandBar" for Sandalwood
- → etc...

YOU COULD USE GEOGRAPHY

All of Juniper Ridge's soaps are branded, "Trail Soaps," with each scented differently. Some of their scent names place them in a particular geographic area:

- → "Mohave Trail Soap"
- → "Sierra Granite Trail Soap"
- → "Big Sur Trail Soap"

Your options are endless. The names you come up with, both the actual name of the commodity product (i.e. "soap") and the various scent (or other characteristic) varieties within the product, are yours to dream up based on the branding scheme you've conjured. As always, think funky, weird, outlandish or daring. Think cohesion, enticement and creative.

PRODUCT DESCRIPTIONS

Once you develop the perfect product names, you must create the perfect product descriptions. Lackluster product descriptions can absolutely destroy your chances of success. A well-written product description has the power to move your customers to a final sale. This is true of online retail, in-person or business-to-business (wholesale). By injecting creativity and product benefits into your product description, your business becomes more likely to convert the casual browser.

While most online customers make their purchase decision on the product picture, the product description helps fill in the gaps to determine if the product is the right fit for them. By educating customers on the key benefits, unique value proposition, and offering a solution to a frustrating problem, your product description can help drive more sales.

SO, WHAT IS A PRODUCT DESCRIPTION?

A product description is the [perfect, edited] copy that describes the features and benefits of your soap and skin care products to a customer. The goal of your product descriptions is to provide the customer with enough information to compel them to want to buy the product immediately. To write a product description that converts, you need to write copy that *persuades* customers to buy. Entice them! What problem does your product solve? What does your customer gain from using your product? What separates your products from others on the market? Your product description needs to answer these questions in a way that is easy to read and within the confines of legalities. Let's look at some examples from companies both inside and outside of our direct industry:

→ Company: Juniper Ridge | Product: Mojave Trail Soap

The Story

A wildharvested fragrance experience from the High Desert of Southern California. A concentrated liquid soap that transforms your shower into a desert oasis. Petrochemical-free, the Mojave Trail Soap is a light hit of the wilderness, designed on the trail and distilled around the campfire. An aromatic snapshot of life on the trail...

Scent Notes

Complex, resinous, earthy: High desert wildflowers at dawn after last night's lightning storm. Desert Cedar bloom with the windows rolled down, cruising at 45 mph across the desert at sunset.

I don't know about you, but I think that is simply amazing. Their "scent notes" section is absolutely incredible: *"Complex, resinous, earthy: High desert wildflowers at dawn after last night's lightning storm. Desert Cedar bloom with the windows rolled down, cruising at 45 mph across the desert at sunset."*

Most importantly, their product descriptions match what they are all about. Everything is cohesive. The name of the product and the product description is unified, consistent and tantalizingly inviting.

→ Company: Burt's Bees | Product: Fabulously Fresh Peppermint & Rosemary Body Wash

There's nothing like a shower to get you going. That's why you're gonna love the energizing, minty-fresh feeling of this body wash. Made with natural Peppermint and Rosemary, this gentle plant-based cleansing formula is the perfect start to any day of your week.

- → Energizes with Peppermint
- → Cleanses gently with Peppermint and Rosemary
- → Fresh scent

Made from the Mediterranean peppermint plant, Peppermint Oil is famous for its cooling effect on skin. You can thank the Menthol for that. Great in baths and facial treatments, it cleanses and tones while helping purify your skin and pores.

Burt's Bees uses geography and infamy to perpetuate the great effects of Peppermint in this product description. Bullet points are always a nice, easy method to conveying product descriptions.

→ Company: Batty's Bath | Product: Bye-Bye Stress Soap
  - → Blend of lavender, chamomile and a tiny bit of vanilla
  - → Aromatic properties help to alleviate stress and tension
  - → Perfect for the bed-time soak
  - → Aids in the relieving of headaches
  - → 100% natural

You've survived another stressful day, and now it's time for some serious R&R. Wash those worries away with our *limited-edition Bye Bye Stress CP Soap! Tranquilize your senses with benefits of lavender, chamomile and vanilla, a trifecta of calming force. This bar is the champion of choice for that late-night soak, especially on the days where your mind seems to keep running. The aromatic properties of these 3 ingredients are best known for relieving mind and body tension, reducing stress levels and anxiety and inducing quality sleep. As an added bonus, if you're a sessional allergy sufferer, lavender and chamomile had both been known to help relieve sinus pressure and headaches."*

This U.K. company is creating a yearning for you to purchase.

→ Company: Christopher Elbow Chocolates | Product: Blueberry Lavender Chocolate

Our 63% custom gourmet dark chocolate infused with floral lavender oil and studded with dried blueberries. Gluten-Free.

New for 2017, our Blueberry Lavender Bar represents the perfect melding of fruity and floral. Our chocolate bars are made by hand in small batches.

No over-complication. Simple, easy to read and to the point. They are a minimally branded company with minimal descriptions, but that doesn't make them any less effective.

→ Company: Thou Mayest Coffee | Product: Alter Ego Coffee
Silky smooth body with milk chocolate drenched nuttiness. This balanced blend has a consistent flavor profile that is easily extractable as an espresso but shows its versatility brewed, as well.

For me, this simple description screams sophistication.

→ Company: Boulevard Brewery | Product: Kolsch Golden Ale
Using European pilsner malt and malted wheat as a base, American Kolsch is bittered with Magnum hops and features herbal, citrusy and spicy notes from end of boil additions of Tradition, Saaz and Saphir. Pouring golden in color, the aroma is of bready malt punctuated by a slightly minty hop character. With a light to medium mouthfeel, American Kolsch delivers a honey-like malt sweetness that gives way to a crisp clean finish with a touch of lingering citrus/herbal hop flavor.

This description style would work wonders with a soap and skin care company. You can see how much Boulevard Brewery puts an emphasis and importance on the ingredients and where they come from. If this is the route your brand takes, I would look up as many craft breweries as possible to garner more inspiration from their product descriptions. The same goes for small-batch artisan spirits.

MAKE IT FUN

Mastering your product descriptions will require creativity and testing. Don't be afraid to test the format of your product descriptions on your most popular products to learn how to proceed. Writing effective copy requires a bit of experimentation to better connect with your customers. Remember, this is about them, not you. Entice your target market with meaningful product descriptions. And in this context, "meaningful" means in cohesion with all of your other branding efforts thus far, such as company name, mission, vision and values.

But most of all, make it fun. If you can't do this yourself, hire someone who can. I have written many product descriptions—as long as the company had a solidified branding platform—and am available for hire at www.lovinsoap.com if you need.

CHAPTER 7:

YOUR CUSTOMER

A products-based business formed out of a budding idea-turned-dream obviously needs someone to purchase its products. That someone is your customer. Too often we *think* we know who our customers are when we don't *really know* who they are. It is therefore imperative at the early stages of your journey to really understand who you are talking to through all of your company's messages.

THINK NICHE

Even huge corporations can't afford to target everyone. The only way your start-up soap and skin care business can effectively compete with large companies is by targeting a niche market. Please keep in mind that the term, "niche" can still be considered quite sizable as a targeted customer base. Targeting a specific market does not mean that you are excluding people who do not fit your criteria. Rather, target marketing allows you to focus your marketing dollars and brand message on a specific market that is *more likely* to buy from your brand than other, similar brands. This is a much more affordable, efficient, and effective way to reach potential customers and generate business. Trying to be everything to everyone is a recipe for disaster. Finding a niche market starts broadly and narrows as more details are discovered.

Finding exactly who will purchase your products is a big undertaking. It is easy to get caught up in the details, which is why I like to first take a much broader approach and then funnel into more specificity later. With some larger demographic terms listed below, let's figure out not only who has a need for your soap and skin care products, but also who is most likely to buy them.

AGE

Age is an important factor to consider when finding a niche. For example, if you wish for your target niche market to be millennials, your website and social media presence has to be top notch; that is what millennials have come to expect. Or, your target market might lean a bit older, perhaps more family-driven and have a larger income than millennials. In this case, more standard advertising and marketing might work, such as magazine ads and promotions, standard mail solicitations, etc. In other words, the older demographic would not require as much focus on a highly-functioning website compared to one targeted for millennials.

LOCATION

Geodemographics, the science of defining population traits by studying the demographics of targeted areas, is an incredible way to deepen the understanding of who a person (or set of people) is and what they want, by taking a closer look at where they live. It is an easy concept to understand; people who live in the same area often have more similar characteristics. There are also similarities in preferences, income levels and backgrounds. Furthermore, a specific neighborhood or town with a certain average income level and population will very likely have people with identical characteristics to a different town that happens to have the same average income level and population, even if they are in an entirely different state. If Town A in Georgia is identified as blue-collar with a median household income of $35,000, Town B in South Carolina with the same blue-collar identity and same median household income will have the same characteristics and buying habits as the people in Town A. This is a phenomenal concept when targeting specific places in the country (or world).

Furthermore, geodemographics can be utilized not only by looking at income, but overall lifestyle. Having spent a little bit of time in the Pacific Northwest in cities like Portland and Seattle, I find that Earth-driven consumerism is much stronger than it is where I live in Kansas City, Missouri. There is an established base of people in the Pacific Northwest who strongly support natural products, sustainable packaging and companies with a strong cause-marketing program. If I were to brand a soap and skin care company according to these principles, I know my market potential in these areas would be greater than in Midwestern cities.

If you want to have some fun with geodemographics, visit the free tool, *Claritas | MyBestSegments* (httpps://segmentationsolutions.nielsen.com/mybestsegments), and use the ZIP Code lookup to find out how a neighborhood is categorized. For example, I can quickly find out the following facts about my ZIP Code, 64105:

- → Population: 4,197
- → Median Age: 29.7
- → Median Income: $45,600
- → Consumer Spend ($/HH): $28,764

Based on my zip code, which is an up-and-coming downtown neighborhood, we see that the median age of the entire accounted-for population within the ZIP code is just 29.7, which is quite young compared to many neighborhoods. This means that young professionals are living in the area. If I had a soap and skin care company that catered specifically to millennials through quality, media-driven websites and social media campaigns, I could target-market this neighborhood through social media campaigns and local newspaper/magazine advertisements with a much greater chance of garnering customers than I could where my parents live, ZIP code 64086:

- → Population: 23,278
- → Median Age: 38.2
- → Median Income: $83,200
- → Consumer Spend ($/HH): $45,942

Even though the population is much higher in this ZIP code, the median age and income suggests an older audience, which might not be in tune with a company driven by youth and technology. Do you see how location (geodemographics) can help you find your niche market?

→ Geodemographics helps to focus on the consumers you're trying to target and then tailor messages, promotions, and products specifically to their interests.

→ Geodemographics helps to find out *where* current customers and prospects live and locate more people like them, across the country…birds of a feather.

→ With geodemographics, you can quickly group similar segments together and target them with similar messaging, ensuring greater efficiency in your marketing campaigns.

Keep in mind that with today's technology and marketing innovation, you can geo-locate a specific target audience, even if your sole revenue stream is online sales. If you have ever engaged in a sponsored advertisement on Facebook, for example, you know that you can opt for geo-locating the advertisement into an area that you deem a hotbed for consumer potential. This is true for most all social media platforms, as well as larger advertisement campaigns, such as Google. Again, the free online geodemographics tool, *Claritas | MyBestSegments* is an incredible resource for finding nationwide demographic clues that will help you find your specific customers in every state, county, city, town, etc.

GENDER

When considering gender as a subset of a targeted niche market, it becomes quite simple. You either direct your message to a majority of one gender or the other, or both. You really only have three options (so don't beat yourself up about it). But, as previously mentioned, be careful and plan ahead (through visualization, mission, vision, values, pen-to-paper, etc.). Trying to direct your message to both can come across as inauthentic if it goes against your brand.

Beauty Brands, for example, does not target men. Yes, they have a few products for men in their stores, but I'm willing to bet that a lot of the male-focused products are still purchased by women (to give to men). Beauty Brands knows who they are, and they aren't going to sway too far away from their targeted market, women.

DON'T MAKE GENDER-SPECIFIC TARGET MARKETING ASSUMPTIONS

After launching The Imperial Drifter, I *assumed* that men, ages 25-60, were to be my specific, targeted demographic. I was selling very high-end products with high prices, and the branding was obviously geared towards men. It was a no-brainer. I didn't feel the need to delve into customer demographics or market research.

I was wrong. The majority of our sales (well over 50 percent) came from women.

The simple fact is, women account for *85 percent* of all consumer purchases including everything from autos to health care:

- → 91% of New Homes
- → 66% PCs
- → 92% Vacations
- → 80% Healthcare
- → 65% New Cars
- → 89% Bank Accounts
- → 93% Food

- → 93 % OTC Pharmaceuticals
- → 58% of Total Online Spending

Whether you plan on focusing intensely on a men's line or not, these statistics do not lie. Keep this in mind.

INCOME LEVEL

Unless your economies of scale (see my book, *Pricing Handmade Soap for Profit*) can match that of a very large soap manufacturer, you are probably not going to be directly competing with the big companies on price. It would be foolish to try. Thus, your soaps and skin care products will be priced higher than commercially mass-produced soaps and skin care products because they cost more to produce than the more economical products manufactured by larger companies.

Accordingly, it would be wise to target a demographic market that has disposable income. This sounds obvious, but I have encountered many who want to promote their handcrafted products as "affordable" and "inexpensive," because they themselves shop for affordable and inexpensive items. But, you are not necessarily your customer; therefore, your personal buying habits should not be factored into how you price your products, and ultimately who you attract. Though customers in all segments value price, when choosing skin care products, the higher the earner the more willing they are to shop by *more than just price*. They will allow themselves to be funneled into a purchase through marketing aesthetics and experience.

Both the Bureau of Labor Statistics and the U.S. Census Bureau have free statistical data that can offer insight into the pricing behaviors of populations in the United States. I encourage you to peruse both sites to get a macro view of economic behavior, and then scale into states, cities, and even neighborhoods to find income-level trends.

EDUCATION LEVEL

An individual's level of education and associated earnings profoundly influence spending patterns. There is usually a direct parallel between education and income. Generally, the higher the education level, the higher the income. We also know through simple census data that if an individual makes more, they spend more in all expenditure categories, including personal care items such as soap and skin care products.

MARITAL OR FAMILY STATUS

This is an interesting one. The demographics are rapidly changing in this demographic subset. Census data tells us that individuals are waiting to get married much, much later than conventional data indicates. Never-married single people ages 25 to 34 now *outnumber* the married crowd in the same age range. This is a stark reversal from just 15 years ago, according to an analysis of new Census data by the Population Reference Bureau.

In essence, selling to singles no longer means just targeting teens and those in their early 20s.

Freed from the occasional financial restraints of family life, singles have a reputation for splurging. They have more money to spend on themselves and they're more willing to indulge on products and services. This is true for both men and women, and all industries are taking note. McDonald's, for example, used to be *very* family-driven in their marketing and advertising efforts. Television commercials and printed materials depicted everything from happy meals, to a smiling Ronald McDonald to mom and dad sharing french fries. But now, you will often see commercials featuring solo diners pounding a Big Mac. McDonald's will always be about family, but being the genius promotors that they are, they've reached an understanding that there's a single population that they should also be targeting.

So, does it matter how soap and skin care products are marketed to singles versus married couples? As of yet, I think the new, older-singles phenomenon is too young to really know. Generally speaking, beauty products are purposely nebulous about marital status. But, if your brand is female driven, with powerful phrases, statements and visuals that suggest independence, autonomy and high self-esteem, you might draw in this growing demographic of singles-with-money whether you mean to or not.

The overall point is, traditional wisdom suggests that all singles want to be married. This notion is not true, and we as business owners must be careful not to put off singles who don't engage in "matrimania," the assumption that all that singles want to do is find a mate.

PSYCHOGRAPHICS

Now that we've covered the larger, macro-demographic subsets, it is time to explore in deeper detail the *minds* of a particular niche market with psychographics. Psychographics include the more personal characteristics of a person or persons.

PERSONALITY

Optimists tend to take chances on new products. Conservative personalities tend to stick with what they know. Some nervous personalities might be too consumed with other life circumstances to care about your soap and skin care products. Other nervous folks might find your products as an escape from their normal routine. It's a crapshoot.

Personalities, as a standalone demographic subset, are not really enough to base a niche market around, but that doesn't mean they shouldn't be considered. Let's say you own a storefront in a touristy location. Now think about your potential customer; inherently they are experiential people, as they are probably outside of their normal routine, made a time, energy and financial commitment to be in your area and obviously appreciate new occurrences. These type of people, with an experimental, valiant outlook on life, are probably going to be a great customer for you.

ATTITUDE

Close your eyes and picture what a typical Dove or Ivory soap shopper looks like in the grocery store. What are they wearing? What else do they have in their grocery cart? What is the look they carry on their face?

What kind of attitude do they have?

Now, close your eyes again and picture what you see as typical shoppers of *your* soap and skin care products. Do this exercise even if you've never had a customer before. If you don't like some aspect of your products, picture them perfect in every way and picture your imagined shoppers. What does your customer look like? What are they wearing? What store are they picking up your product in? Are they getting anything else? What is the look they carry on their face?

What kind of attitude do they have?

After doing this exercise, I'm willing to bet that both pretend shoppers had a different attitude. Try to explain that to yourself. Sure, we did a bit of profiling, but it was perfectly healthy and within the confines of finding the right customer. The overall point of this exercise is to take into consideration the *attitude* of your pretend shopper and see how that attitude is different from your pretend Dove and Ivory shopper. Then, capitalize your marketing messages, advertising and promotions to cater to the attitude of *your* customer.

VALUES

In the previous "location" section, I mentioned that after spending a little time in the Pacific Northwest, I noticed a burgeoning trend towards natural, Earth-driven consumerism. For example, people in cities like Seattle and Portland are far more inclined to bring their own tote bags to grocery stores (so as not to use plastic or paper bags), recycle, purchase locally grown and harvested food and even go as far as caring deeply about *how* a product is packaged (plastic wrap vs. compostable stock paper, or labels printed with soy ink instead of standard ink, which contains petroleum, etc.). In contrast, rural people in the Appalachian foothills are less inclined to care as much about these aspects of consumerism (Please note that I'm not attempting to disparage any segment of society. I offer this example in the same way I would offer up the fact that more trucks are purchased by rural and suburban people than by urban-dwellers. It is a simple, demographic concept that is backed by statistical data).

In this example, a *value-system* system has developed in that part of the country that differs from the value systems in other parts of the country.

So, what set of values does your company wish to live up to, and do these values match up with your targeted customer base?

INTERESTS

Interests are shaped by the surrounding culture, socioeconomic status, the current economy, one's upbringing, and one's self-identity.

The concept of *interest* refers to the ways that a person interacts with the world around him/her. For example,

- → As of this writing, Amanda is almost 30 weeks pregnant. In a little over 10 weeks, I will be a parent for the first time. I have a deep-seated *interest* in raising him or her, caring for him or her, and providing a good upbringing for them. I will continue to look for information that will help make me a better parent. I will spend time learning about being a parent, thinking about being a parent, and of course, interacting with my child.

- → I am also *interested* in becoming wealthy. Though by my own definition I consider myself to be a person of wealth, I am still *interested* in the lifestyles and attitudes of other wealthy people. I will continue to gain information that will help me build more wealth, simply because I'm *interested* in it.

- → I am *interested* in physical achievements. I watch my weight like a hawk. I have a certain physique that I strive for. This *interest* characterizes what I eat, how I spend my time, and where I go.

- → I am *interested* in partying. Sometimes, all I want to do is hang out with friends, get hammered, and have a good time.

Keep in mind that a person's interests change over time. The person who is, at one point in her life, interested in kayaking might, years later, not have as much interest in this activity. Furthermore, there is no single interest that will characterize your target audience. Instead, you'll encounter a spread of interests, depending on who it is that you're targeting and the style and uniqueness of your brand.

Interests can also include markets that they are willing to engage in outside of what you are doing with your business. For example, if your company utilizes essential oils to scent products, your customer is probably also being targeted by essential oil companies. So, look to them to see what they are doing. Look at their style and messaging to see if you can glean anything from them. Or, if your company is branded super chic and stylish, look to other brands (clothing, interior design, etc.) and magazines that target that customer's interests and see what you can discover to capitalize on what you are doing.

ACTIVITIES

Every person on the planet has some activity that they spend time on. What are the activities of your niche market? What does your perfect customer like to do?

- → Fishing
- → Surfing
- → Reading
- → Minecrafting
- → Stamp collecting
- → Pinteresting

- → Online gaming
- → Traveling
- → Craft brewing
- → Gardening
- → Cycling
- → Hiking
- → Painting

The list is potentially endless. However, the more information you gain, the greater you'll understand your particular audience's interests.

You may start to learn, for example, that a huge number of your customers are interested in developing craft boards on Pinterest. They absolutely *love* it. They spend time on the site, making sure each of their unique boards is cohesive, having all of their pins pinned in the right board, etc. They basically breathe Pinterest and take a lot of action towards fun, crafty projects and implementations that inspire them.

Do you think this would have an impact on how you market your products? Where you sell your products? What images you place on your ads? What websites you re-target? What Facebook ad settings you adjust?

Of course it does!

LIFESTYLE

A really fun method to comprising your perfect customer's lifestyle is to create a "day in the life" storyboard.

Assuming you have a rough idea of who your customer's unique style is based, you can really dig into the details of your perfect customer's daily life. Map out their entire schedule, essentially describing what they do and when. Use sticky notes and plaster a wall with them. Make it visual.

The advantage of doing this is that you have a complete overview of your customer's daily life. You can now figure out (and experiment with) how and when to inject your company into their lives. You can figure out when to interrupt people and have it be as seamless and painless as possible.

RESEARCH + INTENT + LOGISTICS

As a general rule, you as the business owner should *constantly* be researching market trends. Watching the latest trends, finding out who is the target of the latest trends and then drawing in your own company's flavor and appeal is vital to establishing a customer base. Furthermore, once you establish a customer based on the latest trends and demographics, you must instate the logistics for them to purchase. It isn't enough to merely establish who your customer is. You must also cater how you advertise, promote and ultimately sell to them with the patterns that your particular demographic is accustomed to.

My parents, both in their 70s, will probably never utilize bank apps that allow you to deposit checks by taking a picture of the check with your phone. I, on the other hand, have not had to go into the bank in years because I utilize this technology. This is a perfect example of research + intent + logistics. The app developer, on behalf of the bank, researched who would be utilizing this technology and found that a younger audience would be more prone to use it versus an older audience. They further catered to a younger audience with their advertisements (a younger person is seen taking a picture of a check on his phone). Then, the product obviously being a phone application, used the logistics of both Android and Apple app platforms to offer the product as a download, a concept most utilized by a younger audience. This is a great example of how the app developers *knew* their customer base. Once you choose exactly who your customer demographic is, *you must cater to their buying habits.* You must make it easy for them to purchase.

RESEARCH!

If you don't know your customer, then you don't know your business. And because it's so hard to hang on to customers you don't intimately know, you will forever be chasing new ones. When you are constantly chasing new customers, because you don't have a loyal following, you get stressed out. When you get stressed out, you get burned out. Speaking from experience as a business owner who has been burned out before, it takes a toll on every other aspect of your life. It sucks, but it can be avoided.

When it comes to planning ahead, an *empirical* understanding of your customer beats gut instinct almost every time. It is time to get facts. It doesn't matter how good you feel about your company's future prospects if you don't take the time to research the market. You might be unknowingly sitting on a gold mine with one of your products, but never know it simply because you didn't seek the right people to be purchasing from you.

If you are baffled about how to conduct market research, begin with some very simple online tools to find out who is currently coming to your website or social media platforms, and how to capitalize on the data.

FACEBOOK

Unlike in days past, it is getting more difficult for people to actually see your business page on their feed, but it is still a vital component to your marketing efforts. And, it provides insight.

In your Facebook business page, click on "insights," and then click on "people." This alone will provide you with some fantastic age and gender demographics, along with geolocation of your largest following.

TWITTER

After logging in, jump to https://ads.twitter.com. Click on "analytics," and then "followers." You might find similar information on Twitter as on Facebook, but keep in mind that the majority of Twitter users are male, so the demographics might look different from your Facebook analytics. This alone offers insight into how you can target a specific market simply by the platform a potential customer is using.

ALEXA

Once your website gets some traffic, you can usually find a listing for it in Alexa.com. Alexa is an incredibly in-depth way to garner more traffic to your site, but more importantly, find out who exactly is interested. Though this is a pay-for-play, I would advise trying their 7-day free trial just to see what it can offer you.

https://www.alexa.com/

GOOGLE ANALYTICS

Google analytics is an unbelievable free tool to find out who is visiting your website. No matter the website platform you use for your website (WordPress, Shopify, Wix, etc…), you can easily plug in Google Analytics to start keeping track of almost every demographic subset you can imagine.

https://analytics.google.com/analytics/web/

THINK WITH GOOGLE

"Think with Google" is an invaluable free resource from Google that allows you to understand the shifts in consumer behaviors, needs, and beliefs to help you unlock fresh insights to drive your business.

https://www.thinkwithgoogle.com/

AMERICAN FACT FINDER

American Fact Finder is a resource for searching U.S. census data. You can filter by age, income, year, race, and location.

http://factfinder.census.gov/faces/nav/jsf/pages/index.xhtml

COUNTY BUSINESS PLATFORMS

County Business Patterns provides information on the areas of the country with large numbers of various types of businesses.

http://www.census.gov/econ/cbp/

NIELSON MYBESTSEGMENTS

Nielsen's MyBestSegments provides you with tools to understand an area's demographics and lifestyle habits. You can find which areas would be most receptive to a campaign or launch, and trends in the areas that have shifted.

https://segmentationsolutions.nielsen.com/mybestsegments

SURVEYMONKEY

Don't underestimate the power of a poll. If you can reach a large enough online audience that will honestly abide by your polling questions, you can garner some great insight into your customer base.

https://www.surveymonkey.com/

YOUR PERFECT CUSTOMER

Don't take this concept lightly. There is a perfect customer for you. In fact, in many ways you *create* your perfect customer by first building an incredible brand with an incredible story, mission, vision, values and aesthetic. When all of these are in place, you can immediately see in your mind's eye the perfect customer. Then you simply find where that customer lives, which will lead to you where likeminded people are living across the country (and world). You will know where they shop, what they eat, how they enjoy their weekends and who they spend time with. All of this data can then be used to cater to their shopping needs. The information available to us is incredible, so use it to reach out to your perfect niche market.

CHAPTER 8:

PRODUCT VARIATION & REVENUE STREAMS

Let me start by saying that I don't know everything. I know, I know...you probably thought otherwise (please soak in the sarcasm)!

What I mean is that you should ultimately choose your revenue streams and product variations based on your furthered research and gut instinct. If you want to engage in craft shows and market events around the clock, more power to you. Just because I lean towards not doing that (as you will soon read), doesn't mean you have to lean that same way. All situations and circumstances are different and should be researched and planned for based on each's own merit and your own preparation.

Furthermore, I advise you to consider and even engage in *all* revenue streams to see what works. For example, as you will read, I'm not the biggest fan of selling via consignment, based on the financial merits of the endeavor, but I'm not saying to *never* participate in consignment if you feel strongly about it. Keep your options open and trust your instincts.

THIS CHAPTER

This chapter is not so much about how to sell within each revenue stream discussed, but rather how each revenue stream you engage in will influence the number of products you can and should craft and not to run your company or yourself into the ground, especially if you are in the solopreneur stage of business. Throughout this chapter, think in terms of products-produced-per-company-member. The more products produced, the larger the burden on each member, and if you are the only member, it all falls on you. Handcrafting products is easy. Keeping track of all pieces of production, marketing and then selling is the hard part and should warrant more of your time than anything else, even production. Therefore, *really* thinking through your product offerings—both what and how many—is a vital piece to your success.

Choosing your revenue streams based on your product variety is a vital piece of information to have written down. This requires you to again start thinking of the [much] bigger picture. Let's break down any and all potential revenue streams and how they relate to your product variety:

REVENUE STREAM & PRODUCT VARIETY:

CRAFT SHOWS & MARKET EVENTS

It goes without saying that typical startup soap and skin care handcrafters love making product. And so, they make tons of product. Being a solopreneur, as is often the case for many (especially early on), they simply cannot control their creative side's relentlessness, so they craft upwards of 35,000 different varieties of soap and probably 50,000 other body care items in any given stretch of time.

Okay, maybe not that much.

But it's a lot. They just can't help themselves. And, as is often the case early on, their main source of revenue is from their own selling table at local or regional events, offering a wide variety of product variation.

Before we go on, let's briefly go over the term, "product variation."

Devoid of quoting some fancy definition, product variation is as simple as this: If you make six different bars of soap (different by name, scent and/or appearance), you have a product variety of six within your product category, soap.

Or, if you have three different bath soaks (different by name, scent and/or appearance), you have a product variety of three within your product category, bath soaks.

To reiterate the above example,

Product category: Soap

  → Product variation (six varieties):

    1. Lavender
    2. Herbs & Flowers

3. Sweet Rose

4. Vetiver

5. Neroli

6. Pizza Sauce

Product category: Bath soaks

→ Product variation (three varieties):

1. Peppermint

2. Rosemary

3. Tequila

Okay, back to the maniacal soapmaker who crafts thousands and thousands of different product varieties…

A LARGE PRODUCT VARIATION IS GOOD FOR MARKETS

When selling at a craft show or market event, having a large product variety certainly seems appealing, no question. It is enticing for a show attendant or passerby to have so much choice. I understand this approach, and if this is what you would like to engage in long term, more power to you.

Alas, solely selling at craft shows and market events will probably not create enough profit for you to make a living, but that is not necessarily the rule. Don't get me wrong, I have seen very successful vendors who work just about every weekend at various events, and they make a good living. That said, it is often by selling merchandise that yields higher margins than soap. Personally, I see craft shows and market events as a means to advertise and promote my company, as opposed to being there just to garner sales.

Allow me to demonstrate some simple example numbers to see what a rough estimate of profit would be for a craft show-only seller:

A soapmaker, let's call her Paige, engages in 30 different craft shows and market events for one calendar year (which is a lot, considering there are only 52 weekends in a year). After adding up all the booth fees from all 30 events, the total cost comes to $7,500 (roughly $250 booth fee cost per event).

Paige's economies of scale (see my book, *Pricing Handmade Soap for Profit*) has reached a point in which her average soap bar cost in raw materials is $1.25. She sells them for $7 per bar. This is an initial gross profit of $5.75 per bar, before any other expenses are accounted for.

Thus, Paige now knows that just to break even on the craft shows and market events for the year, she will have to sell 1,305 bars of soap ($7,500 / $5.75 = 1,304.34), which comes to 44 bars per event (1,305 bars / 30 events = 43.5 bars). Again, this is just to break even on the cost of the events. We haven't yet included salaries, all other overheads, marketing costs, office supplies, travel, merchant account fees, taxes, etc.

Now, let's say Paige sells an average of 200 bars per event, with her gross profit margin for each bar being the $5.75 previously mentioned. This equates to $1,150 per event, which totals $34,500 in sales over 30 events. We must then take the cost of the booth fees out, which brings the sales number down to $27,000.

This $27,000 is Paige's total sales minus booth fees, minus raw materials. In other words, we have only taken out *two expenses*; raw materials and booth fees. There are a host of unaccounted for expenses that must still be taken out of this number. And even if there *weren't* any more expenses to take out (which is ridiculously impossible), Paige probably doesn't want to live off of $27,000 a year. The reality is, after taking out all other expenses and retaining some business savings, she might be able to afford a salary of maybe $7,000 tops. This is an incredible amount of work for a small financial retribution.

CRAFT SHOWS & MARKET EVENTS AS A REVENUE STREAM:

Advantages:

- → Product variety for any particular product category can be large showcasing creativity and offering choice
- → Quick way to earn cash flow

Disadvantages:

- → Hard work, laborious, and often unreliable
- → Generally, not a large payout based on workload

HIGH PRODUCT VARIATION

If craft shows and market events are going to be your choice as a primary revenue stream, make all the different product varieties you wish. Have at it! I believe that craft shows and market events warrant a high variation in products.

With selling at craft shows and market events, be advised that your workload versus your potential payout might be quite different from other revenue streams. Furthermore, it becomes more and more difficult to keep track of inventory with so many different products, not to mention their exact cost per ounce/gram.

As a general rule, especially if you are just starting out, I would engage in a few craft shows and market events simply to see how they go, create exposure for your company and garner some quick cash flow for your business. I would also go into each event knowing that you are there primarily to advertise and promote your company and not to expect huge sums of income.

Before I opened my storefront, we were mainly a wholesale-driven company. That was our revenue stream of choice. But, inevitably we would still make what we wanted to make and when we wanted to make it, so we always had still-to-be-sold product lying around in our workshop. Based on the amount of inventory that gathered, we would then plan for a local event to sell off all these marginal products (marginal to our wholesaling endeavors) at a discounted price, with the primary motive of creating quick cash flow from secondary products, as well as advertise and promote our company. Thus, craft shows and market events were not our primary revenue stream; they were more an easy manner in which to create cash flow when needed and tidy up our inventory.

REVENUE STREAM & PRODUCT VARIETY:

WHOLESALE

I wrote a book recently titled, How to *Wholesale Your Handcrafted Soap*. You can find it on Amazon. So, I'm not going to go into a frenzied pitch on the detailed logistics of wholesaling here, but I will certainly relate how it can affect your company's *product variety*. But first, a homily on keeping track of your costs:

EVERY PENNY COUNTS

Knowing your costs for every product you create is your most important responsibility as a business owner in this industry. This cannot be overstated, whether you wholesale or not.

One of the best things that a soap and skin care business owner can do is keep accurate records of business operations, especially manufacturing and sales. Unfortunately, I see much disregard for the true significance of doing this in our industry, but I also understand why. Generally speaking, the disregard to keep formal, precise records of batches made with all associated costs is because most of us in this industry start out as artful hobbyists; we do not feel the need to keep documented records of each batch, detailed notes about any waste, the exact yields, or the ease in which we might have to scale up a beautifully designed swirl, etc. We are creatives first and businesspeople second. Unfortunately, many of us don't break this mindset even after deciding to proceed with a business.

You must switch priorities if you really want to make your living from making and selling your products. You must be a businessperson first and a creative second, unless you can totally delegate the recording of all manufacturing accounting to someone you trust immensely. But even then, you still must make the decision as to whether a certain product is worth producing at a specific cost.

Doing this becomes even more important if you decide to engage in wholesaling. Most products-based businesses that collapse do so because the producers fail to keep quality records of their goods, period. Essentially, they sell their products at too low a price, which slowly eats profits until there is nothing left.

Keeping records will help you determine profits. If we are really going to get down to it, the main goal of having a business is to make profits. The profits made cannot, however, *even be seen* if the business owner fails to look at their true production costs. This is why more time must be spent on determining the production costs *of each product crafted* and then decide whether the company can actually engage in wholesaling (or, for that matter, any other type of selling). This, inevitably, will also affect how big or small your product line should be.

I will often get emails from budding soapreneurs with some rendition of this subject header: HOW MUCH SHOULD I CHARGE WHOLESALE?

They go on to write something like, "My bar weighs four ounces and I'm trying to wholesale to some local stores. How much should I charge?"

Well, *how the hell should I know*?

There is absolutely no way of me knowing the answer to this question without knowing more! For instance, *exactly* how much does your product cost to make based on ingredients? How much, in quantity, are you purchasing in raw materials? Are you purchasing coconut oil by the jug or by the barrel? What, exactly, is your waste factor? So your bar weighs four ounces, great. Is it comprised of four ounces of organic materials, dusted with 24 carat gold? Or, is it crafted from 4 ounces of saponified soybean oil? Can you see how this might make a difference in cost and thus pricing?

I will ask them how much their product costs to make. They usually don't know, or they will give me a range. Having a guestimate, or range is not knowing. Knowing your costs for every product you create is your most important responsibility as a business owner in this industry. This cannot be overstated.

HOW TO KEEP TRACK

If you want to count your pennies (wholly recommended), you will probably need to invest in a software program. Remember, establishing your costs for every product you create is your most important responsibility, so it will inevitably take up much of your time and energy. That said, you might as well make it as easy as possible. In my opinion, the easiest way to keep track of all your costs is through utilizing a software program.

SOAPMAKER

I highly recommend utilizing the downloadable, "Soapmaker" program from https://www.lovinsoap.com. It is incredibly affordable for what the program offers.

CRAFTY BASE

Another option is the online-only, "Crafty Base" program from https://craftybase.com/. It does everything that Soapmaker does, but instead of a one-time purchase and download, you pay monthly for your subscription.

QUICKBOOKS

The "standard" version of QuickBooks is constructed in a way that assumes either a service-based business or a buy-and-resale business, where the company purchases goods at a wholesale price and sells them at a retail price. You are not buying your soap wholesale and then reselling it, you are making it. Therefore, obtaining the appropriate version of QuickBooks, such as their "Manufacturing" version is advised. Be informed, the manufacturing version of QuickBooks is quite expensive compared with the two programs above.

MICROSOFT EXCEL (OR OTHER SPREADSHEET-STYLE PROGRAMS)

Yes, you can keep track of your costs through excel, but it is challenging. Remember that the cost of raw materials changes from season to season, year to year, depending on the quality of the harvest. The three programs above take care of this for you, as you simply input the cost of every raw material you purchase in real time, and over time, the program(s) will automatically average the cost from every purchase. This is incredibly difficult with a spreadsheet style method, unless you are very well trained in the program.

Okay, back to wholesaling and product variety...

WHOLESALING AND PRODUCT VARIETY

As mentioned, if you engage in many different craft shows and local/regional market events, a high product variety can be to your advantage. These types of shoppers love to see the plethora of varieties you have to offer. Wholesaling is much different.

Let me preface this by saying that if your company has reached effective economies of scale, has a systematic plan in place and know every production unit's cost down to the penny and can manufacture them at a high clip, then you can disregard my following creed. But, if you are just starting out in the wholesale world, or even just thinking about it—especially if you are still in the solopreneur stage—read on to examine the consequences of trying to make and sell too much product variation via wholesale.

As of this writing, I live in Kansas City, Missouri. My beautiful, enterprising town is where we launched Prairie Soap Company, LLC back in 2009. I intended to wholesale our products here in the greater Kansas City metropolitan area, effective immediately.

Not only did I not know my true costs, I was going to directly compete with an indomitable force in the handcrafted soap and skin care industry, Indigo Wild. Indigo Wild, producers of the cottage-industry famed "Zum bars," are located right here, in the heart of Kansas City. In a previous downtown apartment I inhabited, I could have walked to their operation facility. Then and now, you couldn't ask a stranger on the street about Indigo Wild without them knowing.

My admiration and respect for Indigo Wild cannot be explained through the written word. They are doing it right in, seemingly, every way, and I can surmise through seeing it firsthand that their profits are ever-growing. If you do not know who I am speaking of, feel free to check them out at https://www.indigowild.com. And while you're there, read every page! See how cohesive their company messages are. See how their branding plays into everything they do!

Considering they are a sizeable, local handcrafted soap and skincare company, I naively assumed that I had to compete with Indigo Wild on *product variation*, not considering how large a company they had become, allowing themselves recurrent product-line expansion over time. But, I was too naïve to care. If they were going to wholesale a million different varieties of soap, not to mention a host of other skincare products, I was going to do the same.

Okay, maybe not a million. But they were selling a lot.

At the time, most groceries and boutiques that parlayed with Indigo Wild generally carried twenty or more soap varieties with a host of bodycare products to complement. Nowadays, it is often much more.

Making and selling twenty different soaps didn't sound like a lot to me, as I was young, energetic and full of a hunger that could only be satisfied by directly competing with who I knew to be a worthy and admirable local business rival. I decided that we were going to sell 18 different soaps. What I failed to consider was the scale in which Indigo Wild was selling, and, eventually, the scale in which *I* was to sell.

My wholesale package to any local grocer or boutique was 12 units per variety. With a product variation of 18, this amounted to 240 bars of soap (18 x 12 = 240). Before engaging in this strategy, I knew that I would need larger molds, so I borrowed some money to purchase them. We acquired molds large enough to make 120 bars at a time.

So, we were off. I was selling pretty consistently into local chain grocers and health markets. I knew that if I could get into one Hy-Vee store (local chain grocery), I could get into all of them, as the chain operates through the whole of the Midwest. Our initial purchases were fantastic. I never realized how much money we could make on first-time purchases! It was a wonderful feeling to be making and selling that much product. Our customer base continued to grow, and for a short while, we were directly competing with Indigo Wild.

Until we couldn't keep up, and our stuff wasn't selling.

First of all, I was worn thin. At the time, I still did not have any employees, only a sales rep. Thus, my days were crammed with making large batches of soap all day long. And, because we offered so many varieties (based on our company size at the time), our raw materials were spread thin. When it was time to purchase raw materials, the purchases were sizeable, which often inhibited our cash flow. The company was spread thin, and I was certainly spread thin.

Second of all…

Checking my email one fall morning, about eight weeks after the initial sale to a local health market, I received a note from the buyer, explaining how only a handful of the varieties were selling at a normal rate, and the others were just collecting dust. This same message was eventually repeated by a handful of our newfound retailers. I was horrified!

I was dismayed, thinking that if people weren't buying *all* of my soap varieties, they obviously must not like them all. This, of course, is not true, as our price point offered a one-off approach to purchasing, as opposed to buying a handful as one would a mainstay commodity. I still took it personally. It was hard not to.

In reality, they probably *did* appreciate them all, but could only afford the best of the best. And, whether I liked it or not, I had top sellers and I had bottom sellers. That is how it works in a products-based business.

In an effort to compete with a huge company (Indigo Wild currently has over 300 SKUs!), I spread my company (and myself) too thin. I didn't consider how long it took Indigo Wild to get to where they are now. Indigo

Wild has been around since the mid-90s, and has a plethora of experience in production and selling, and I had literally none at the time. I was just a child in the mid-90s, so I don't have any personal experience with them, but I am willing to bet they didn't start out by wholesaling 300 SKUs. They started out small and grew their product line over time, which is what I should have done.

I learned many lessons about my own ego, the way in which I hastened the making and selling process and ultimately my place (at the time) in the industry. I bit off more than I could chew, so my next bite was of humble pie.

We were forced to trim our product line down to our top eight soaps. By doing this, I had to basically eat the cost (or so I thought at the time, before we had a storefront) of the other 10 beautifully designed boxes that we had professionally printed, equipped with barcodes and all the beauty and simplicity that our company was trying to convey. Yes, not only did we have to purchase larger equipment, but we also purchased thousands and thousands of soap packaging boxes, each printed unique to the 18 different varieties we intended to sell. Again, at the time, cutting out 10 of the 18 varieties (which equated to several thousand boxes) was a huge hit to our company's bottom line.

But, after trimming down to eight soap varieties, we quickly realized it was a smart move. Even though our orders were much smaller in size, quantity and revenue, we actually ended up making *more* money. A lot more. Reorders came in much faster, as *all* the soaps were selling at a high clip, not just a few. We eventually recouped the money spent on soap box packaging, and, thank God, we would eventually, though unforeseen at the time, be able to use those as well.

What's more, we probably could have made *even more* money by cutting our product line down to four or six.

Now, let me be clear. Our 18 soaps were awesome. The 10 I cut did not suck. The situation that forced me to trim my product line was not due to lack of quality, but lack of time related to name recognition in the marketplace and the lack of trust with potential consumers. Instead of starting with eight and working up to 18, I started with 18 and had to downsize to eight.

My company was brand new. The public did not know Prairie Soap Company like they knew Indigo Wild. Indigo Wild had *earned* the trust of our local customer base and grew their product lines over time. Based on the longevity and trust their brand fostered, customers were, and are still, willing to try new things from Indigo Wild. This is what I missed.

If we had started with selling only a small product variety of what I knew to be the best sellers, and did so for a few years before expanding the line, we would have developed a trust with local customers and a healthier financial report with the buying managers of the retail stores we were now in. Another vital piece I was missing was the powerful (and necessary) results of "aftermarketing," discussed in my book, *How to Wholesale Your Handcrafted Soap*.

CREAM OF THE CROP

Much to the dismay of your creative side, there is nothing wrong with wholesaling a small variety of product, at least at first. Please understand that this is not the rule; it really depends on your situation. I broke my own rule in not having a streamlined product variety to suit several stores – stores who *wanted* a surplus of offerings from our company. Those, however, were the exception to the rule. By staying very streamlined with our product line overall, we entered new retail stores easier (less risk on their end with a smaller purchase package) and were taking reorders on a recurrent basis.

WHAT'S WRONG WITH ONE?

Some incredibly lucrative products-based companies thrive by selling just one product. Though this idea may be a shot through your creative heart, I ask you to consider it.

First, think about how dedicated you could be to all other facets of your business, namely accounting and customer service. Not only could you provide the utmost in product quality, there would be zero confusion as to how much it cost and how you could improve on manufacturing costs ongoing, since it is just one single product. Furthermore, since you would be producing only one item, the lion's share of your time could be committed to customer service, which requires intense skills and patience when it comes to wholesale. Lastly, you can approach a "true" wholesale distribution model, in which you sell thousands of your single units to a distributor, and the distributor then sells to the retail store. Doing this with several varieties becomes quite difficult, and distributors typically do not want to mess with too high a variation.

Let's look at a few companies who [by and large] sell just one item.

CROCS

These hilariously-ugly, but super-comfy foam clogs have been a huge hit since they were first released to the public. Over 100 million pairs of

Crocs have been sold to date, and the footwear giant shows no signs of stopping.

SPANX

In the never-ending battle of the bulge, women (and men) have relied heavily on high-quality wear to help make them look their best. Born from the bright idea that by cutting the feet from a pair of panty-hose a woman really can look good under her trousers. Easy-peasy. One item.

MICHELIN

In a day and age where most companies have almost too much going on, Michelin has remained faithful to the cause of strictly manufacturing quality tires.

GORILLA GLUE

In the world of hardware stores and DIY weekenders, Gorilla Glue has become a staple with awesome marketing and advertising, streamlined production and a loyal customer base.

Now, even though crocs mainly sell only one style shoe, they still have to manufacture different sizes and colors. Spanx and Michelin the same. If your company were to sell just one product, you most likely wouldn't have to even do that! Or, even if you did, it might be a minimal difference in size or container size/shape (think Carmex; tube or jar), still easily streamlined in production and sales.

To further this idea, below are a few more pros to selling one (or very few) products:

FOCUS

You get to narrow your focus on creating one truly amazing product. Without all the distractions of building, managing and selling multiple products, you get to really hone the finer details of your primary offering, making it much better than any others in the market. It also allows you razor-sharp focus in your marketing tactics, in selecting the highest quality channels and in sourcing traffic that quickly converts into happy customers.

The last time I waltzed through the retail giant, World Market, I noticed the various soaps for sale. Each soap, individually, was from a different company. In other words, the soap company selling to World Market did not sell a vast product variation. They sold *one* SKU, one soap.

BEING NICHE

You have the ability to be incredibly niche, and instead of building a product that serves all, you can build a product that is aiding an underserved market exceptionally well. Think of a specialized facial bar, or a hilariously branded men's butt crack soap. Targeting a specific sector within the larger market can lead to great success because you will be able to easily capture most in the sector, especially if they feel underserved.

EFFICIENCY

With razor-sharp focus on one product, targeting one type of consumer, you can rapidly develop your product rather than splitting your efforts across multiple channels. In fact, you get to *really know* your customers, becoming more sensitive to their changing needs. At the same time, you become agile enough to repeat your product offering to cater to those needs. This concept cannot be overstated.

So, there you go. Take my advice on wholesaling or leave it. Just keep in mind that when you start really selling your product to a lot of stores, the workload is immense.

REVENUE STREAM & PRODUCT VARIETY:

ONLINE RETAIL

In my estimation, especially in the handcrafted soap and skin care industry, there are two notions pertaining to product variety and success online. The first has been somewhat unveiled to you in the wholesale section; the notion that a smaller, more streamlined product line can have its advantages, especially when just starting out.

The second, which is crucial to selling online, is not so much about product variety being the means to selling, but showing consumers *how* to purchase by navigating through your existing variety. With online retail, especially when attempting to sell consumable, skin-applying smell-goods, you must take your customer's hand and guide them through the process. It's not so much about your product variety (although that does play a role), but how you showcase the variety you have.

YOU MAY NEED TO REDUCE VARIETY

The last time I had a cold and my sinuses were throbbing as if I had a cinder block lodged in my face, I ran up to the pharmacy to find something that would help. The overwhelming number of competing formulas, each slightly different from the other, simply progressed my already aching head. I was faced with twenty different types of cold tablets from a single manufacturer: one for a cold plus sore throat, another for a cold plus nasal congestion, another to be taken only at night, another to be taken during the day. I was suffering and just wanted to feel better, but I was forced to pick and choose what symptoms I had and didn't have. I was being offered "overchoice."

I ended up walking away empty handed, more confused and desperate than when I walked in.

Again, as disclosed in the previous wholesale section, sometimes offering too many choices prompts the confused consumer to defer a purchase or run to the arms of a competitor with a less cluttered product line. Though my own account at the pharmacy was in a brick-and-mortar setting, the same concept applies online. I believe I have expressed the need to reduce product variety enough, so let's focus on the second notion of selling online as it pertains to product variety.

NAVIGATING YOUR CUSTOMER'S CHOICE

Perusing through the vast array of electronics in the retail megastore Best Buy, I came to the computer/laptop aisle. Much like my cold medicine, the choices here seemed endless and overwhelming, especially for someone who doesn't understand the meaning of all the specifications on the neatly displayed, bullet-pointed list of selling points for each machine.

But then I happened upon the Dell brand section and was intrigued by their methods to sell to me. They identified their computers in terms of who they are intended, as opposed to a bullet-point list of specs which didn't make sense to me. There was a "gaming" computer, a "home office" computer, an "internet ready" computer, and so on. Rather than worrying about what specs I required, I was introduced to the machine that met *my* profile and intentions.

I thought this was brilliant and subsequently very much lacking in our cottage industry. Remember, we know all of the industry-specific terminology, but our customers might not. They need to be guided through a sale.

Whether you have a product line of eight or 80, if all your customers have to go by are the pictures, descriptions and overall appearance of the website, the reluctance to make an online purchase will continually rise until they leave your site.

I'll say again, in this method, the focus is not so much on the product variety offered, but the way in which you aid customers in the decision-making process.

To use another example outside of our industry, Titleist, the largest and most successful golf ball producer, in the past five years, has gone from offering an extremely large assortment of golf balls to only five. Furthermore, Titleist, in an array of different methodologies, asked potential purchasers a series of questions, the answers to which would result in the recommendation of a particular golf ball. If you tended to hit far but off-line, a particular ball would be recommended. By relating your tendency to be good around the green but short off the tee, another ball would be recommended. By drastically shrinking its product line and helping consumers navigate their options, Titleist has procured more profits as a whole.

So, how can you capitalize on this method in selling online with soap and skin care?

Maybe it is as simple as divvying up your product line by directing products to a specific skin type or body topography. For example, let's say you decide to have a soap product variation of twelve. You could showcase your variation by specific 'lines' within the same category (soap):

→ The Facial Line (3 varieties)

→ The Body Line (3 varieties)

→ The Exfoliate Line (3 varieties)

→ The Moisturizing Line (3 varieties)

Showcasing your products in this way automatically enhances the user's experience, especially if the presentation is clearly and professionally portrayed on your website. This simple step (done with foresight) would immediately help your potential customers get to where they want to go much faster, which is crucial in today's online shopping atmosphere. You could do the same with scent or appearance.

K.I.S.S. (KEEP IT SIMPLE, SILLY!)

My number one piece of advice is to keep your online storefront simple. I've bludgeoned you over the head enough with the idea of streamlining your products for the benefit of all (mainly for the financial retention of your bottom line, as well as your own stress level), but let's discuss some more reasons, especially pertaining to online retail.

Let me preface by reiterating, as it pertains to online retail and your product line, the importance of following your own desires. If you want to craft dozens and dozens (or hundreds and hundreds) of products for your online store, it is your decision. That said, let's look at how this might affect the true professionalism of your operation:

PRODUCT LINE & PRODUCT PICTURES

Today's consumers are super web-savvy – mobile-enabled data sifters who pounce on whichever brand looks and feels up-to-the-minute and trendy. Brand loyalty is actually on the decline, as there are so many unique and chic options to choose from, especially aesthetically. The dire need for high quality product photography cannot be overstated. Your website will not produce traffic or sales if your product photography sucks, period.

Without a plan, you might start making products left and right, intending to sell *all* of them on your website. If you have the absolute perfect product photography setup and know what you are doing (or know someone who does), you are all set.

What I see more often is inferior product photography, with each photo of a respective product being off-kilter compared to the next, with random lighting settings (a sign that the photos might have been taken at much different times of the day or year), and an overall amateurish look. This is a clear indication that the company owner has not truly thought about a foundational product line that warrants online professionalism and appearance.

And, more often than not, I see this only on sites that offer a huge product line. It is obvious that the product line is too big to keep up with an aesthetically pleasing online shopping experience.

So, what if your products were streamlined to just eight? Or 18? Or 4? Or 32? What if you knew, through intensive planning and writing, that your foundational product line was going to be a set number and would not change (unless absolutely necessary).

You would then get to work crafting each product, packaging them perfectly and finalizing professional product photography for each product in your line. When customers come to your site, they will see your foundational products in all of their proficient glory, as opposed to a slopped-together crusade of various photographs taken at different times from different angles.

The professionalism of your website will live and die by the quality of your product photography. If, in contrast to the example above, you decide to make and sell over 50 or 60 bars online, along with a host of other skin care products, on your own with no help, the chances of you hurling up inferior photography on your site increases exponentially.

Think it through. Think years from now, not weeks from now. What is your online business all about, and how are you going to streamline your offerings into a powerful sales presentation around the clock? The answer to this question is to start small and smart, growing as you experience some sales traction.

QUALITY, NOT QUANTITY

I mentioned that Indigo Wild now sells over 300 SKUs, which is a lot. A whole lot. But, they also have a lot of people on staff. It literally "takes a village" to run a successful soap and skin care business, especially if you want to continually grow product lines. Most people in our industry don't get out of the solopreneur stage of business because they aren't thinking big enough, and they don't have a dedicated plan as to how they will earn their money (dedicated revenue streams with revenue goals).

If you look at how many products you are currently making and selling online and divide it by the number of people operating your business, what would it be? It could be as much as 50 or more if you are doing this by yourself. There is no right or wrong answer to this simple division problem. But, if your online business isn't where it needs to be, perhaps the reason is in the unassuming math you've just done.

Every product you craft needs to be incredibly well thought out from start to finish. Don't just focus solely on the ingredients. Think through the name, the packaging, the branding and design of the labels, the way it will be photographed, etc. If you spend more time, energy and resources on the quality of each individual product, you can streamline your offerings into a smaller set of truly beautiful, abundant merchandise to be sold online or elsewhere.

REVENUE STREAM & PRODUCT VARIETY:

BRICK & MORTAR STOREFRONT

Don't assume that your soap store will be anything like the one I had, or someone else currently has. Even though you may have—or soon want to open—a retail storefront with the primary objective of selling the soap and skin care products that your company crafts, you still might have an immense product assortment that includes merchandise outside of our industry, or at the very least, industry-complementary merchandise.

In other words, no two soap stores are alike, so keep this in mind when it comes to product variation and assortment.

MERCHANDISE MIX

Generally speaking, specialty retailers, which is how your company would be categorized, have a smaller product breadth than a general merchandise store. This, of course, is because their products have a narrower focus and a built-in niche (i.e. soap and skin care). However, they may have an equal, if not wider, product *depth* if they choose to stock a greater variety of each product line. Ultimately, the choice is theirs to make, and there are many factors that go into making that decision.

Yankee Candle, for example, will have a smaller variety (or breadth) of product categories than Walgreens, even if they have the same number of actual units in inventory.

- → Yankee Candle may stock only 20 categories of candles, but they may stock 30 colors and scents of each of those candles (variations).
- → Walgreens stocks 200 different product categories, but may stock only one or two variations, brands or styles of each product.
- → Each company has exactly 2,000 units of inventory in their store.

Obviously, these two stores have completely different strategies for their product assortment because of the needs of their customers, even though they have the exact same number of sellable units.

Data suggests that both fragrance and color are more important to the Yankee Candle customer than having 100 candle *styles* to choose from. On the other hand, convenience is important to Walgreens customers, as they may want to pick up toothpaste and batteries in one stop.

Thus, in a brick and mortar setting, it would be to your company's disadvantage to make only three bars of any particular soap. The three would be purchased quickly, and you would be left with a blank space on your shelf. Depth and variety are both important in a specialized retail store setting.

RETAIL STOREFRONT = HIGH PRODUCT VARIATION

If you decide to engage in a highly specialized soap and skin care retail store, the variation in your products can be quite high, and frankly, should be.

This, perhaps more than any other revenue stream (though not necessarily) is where your creativity is allowed to shine the most. You can saturate your own store's shelves with all your creations, coming up with fanciful and enticing names and visual merchandising techniques.

You will have the ability to create seasonal offerings that will revolve around the calendar year at a faster pace than you might expect. You can, if you so choose, take the advice or request of valuable repeat customers, crafting something fresh to their sensibilities.

Furthermore, whatever specialized product does not sell on a recurrent basis, can be set at a clearance price to get off the inventory books and create a small bump in cash flow. You have the ability to do this simply by having a walk-in storefront. It's all about access.

DON'T GO TOO CRAZY!

The opinion and advice from the previous paragraphs should be taken with a grain of salt. You still have to make a dedicated plan and keep track of inventory on a recurrent basis.

Having a large inventory in a retail storefront is not for the faint of heart. It is really hard work keeping up with everything, and every unit has to be accounted for. As noted in the wholesale section of this chapter, every single bar of soap or skin care product needs to be accounted for—even the mess-ups, the drops, the miss-cuts—everything has a quantitative value that must be documented. Yes, this is an awesome, artful craft, but it is also manufacturing. You are a product manufacturer, so think like one.

PRODUCT COST AND CASH FLOW

With a vast breadth of product variation, you can expect a vast breadth of raw materials. Whether you use synthetic fragrance oils or essential oils, the more variation you offer, the more purchases you will be making towards more smell-goods, both in quantity and assortment. And of course, this applies to materials, beyond fragrance. Carrier oils and butters, colorants, caustics, packaging, etc. will all require more purchasing.

With the seemingly strange lapse in time between making and selling (strange compared to other industries) due to the cure time of soap, planning ahead becomes absolutely necessary. If you are to engage in a retail storefront, I strongly recommend creating a 15-month production plan for the upcoming year, which actually starts three months before the year begins, October. This aids in knowing when you will need to purchase raw materials, thus alleviating some of the inevitable cash flow issues you will face with the seasonality of consumerism in retail.

REVENUE STREAM & PRODUCT VARIETY:

CONSIGNMENT

Consignment is a hot topic for new soapreneurs, and many I meet ask if I think consignment is right for them. There's no simple answer, but there are pros and cons to consignment that you should weigh before making your choice, especially as it relates to product variation.

WHAT IS CONSIGNMENT?

Many store owners, especially smaller boutiques, don't want to take a chance on new product lines right away. Consignment lets them test their market for your soap and skin care product safely (financially speaking), thus having their customers decide. This in itself is one of the pros of consignment. When stores don't have to take a big risk, they are more likely to try your product on their shelves the first time you inquire from a sales perspective.

Selling on consignment also offers you the opportunity to show the storeowner you are confident that your products will be a hit with their customers. When your products do sell, consignment percentages are usually 60-70 percent of the sale price, as opposed to wholesale which is usually 50-60 percent.

The most obvious con to consignment is how unreliable it is, both in actually profiting, and if you do, when you get your money. You don't receive payment for your merchandise until it sells. Thus, much like every other revenue stream mentioned, managing your cash flow carefully becomes extremely necessary.

As far as product variation goes, I lean towards the idea of offering a wide array of product, because often smaller boutiques are in constant need for new items. Having empty space on shelves in retail is a huge no-no, so if you come along with a large product variety for them to fill their shelves, all the better for everyone.

REVENUE STREAM & PRODUCT VARIETY:

ENDLESS OPTIONS!

Ultimately, you get to choose your revenue stream(s) based on what your strengths are as a company and where you want to be financially and otherwise in the foreseeable future. The look, feel and vibe of your company really has to be strongly suited for any given revenue stream, not to mention your willingness to inject foresight into your company's product variation.

If one of your strengths is design and visually aesthetic implementation, focusing heavily on building and designing a beautiful website might be the way to go, thus making your product variation accordingly. Or, if you just love making products around the clock and would rather delegate the other duties to someone else, perhaps wholesale and/or craft shows could be the main focus, thus making your product variation accordingly.

The key takeaway from this chapter is to think through all potential revenue streams before you jump in with two feet. Or, if you have already jumped in, established a company with a name, packaging and labeling, etc., you can always pivot, change and improve on it with your keen sense of foresight. If, when visualizing and writing, you see your products on the shelves of Whole Foods Market across the nation, engage yourself wholeheartedly in wholesaling, and create a product line that suits your vision. If, when visualizing and writing, you see yourself running a beautiful storefront, engage yourself wholeheartedly to doing this, and create a product line that suits your vision, and so on.

Every successful products-based company in the world has a very keen eye on their product line. Prosperous companies delicately balance the invigorating appeal of creativity and sound financial planning when it comes to what products they will manufacture and the variety created within any given product category.

And, as always, think big. If you feel, instinctively, that you are selling too much variation and it is time to cut back on a few, but the one variety you know you need to cut is your neighbor's husbands' favorite so you decide to keep it after all, then you aren't thinking big enough. You will never be able to please everyone with your product line, whether it is vast or very simple. If you have an up-to-date sales history of your products, and you know you need to simplify, just look at the numbers, as they will showcase what needs to be cut. If you don't yet have a clear sales history of your product line, keep going until you start to see a pattern.

CHAPTER 9:

SCALABILITY, HIRING & SALARY

Scalability is one of *the* most important factors for soap and skincare startups hoping to take their current business to the next level. Scalability is your company's ability to handle a growing amount of work, along with its potential to be enlarged to accommodate growth. Good scalability simply means that your business has the potential to multiply revenue with minimal incremental cost.

If you are still spending most of your time working *in* your business, rather than *on* your business, then you are not yet ready to scale. If, in three to five years, you are still making every decision—not to mention every product—your company's scalability potential has not increased.

You must acquire help.

Being a solopreneur in a product-manufacturing industry will get you just so far. There is a ceiling on what you will be able to produce and sell, no matter how proficient you are. Running a manufacturing business is far more involved than making and selling products. You, in effect, must become the greatest problem-solver that ever lived. For example, if you garner a large wholesale customer base, issues will arise. Invoices will get lost. Payments will be forgotten. Shipments will be damaged. Mistakes will be made. You will be spending a lot of time emailing and calling clients to make them happy and to collect your money. All of this becomes part of the job on a daily basis.

You will be required to pay taxes and to keep your inventory of both finished goods and raw materials up to date. You will be required to continually update your website to maintain functionality and attention. Stagnant websites don't generate sales, so you must constantly shake things up with new sales banners, holiday-product teasers and blog posts. You must funnel your clientele into a sale using newsletter marketing campaigns. You must continually research and develop what is needed to stay fresh—whether it be products or your branding—as nothing in business is concrete, so knowing when you need to make changes will play a vital role in your success. Whether you utilize the services of a sales representative or not, your primary function every day should be on sales, not production. You get to eat because of sales. You get to take care of your family because of sales. You get to hire more people because of sales. You get to live the life of your dreams because of sales.

This list of tasks is just a *fraction* of what is required from a manufacturing company. You cannot possibly do all of this by yourself, unless you are okay with very little money in your pocket. Generally speaking, we all start out as lovers of the craft, and so we deem ourselves crafters. But, if you really want to advance yourself into an enterprising role, you might need to start thinking yourself a smart businessperson and not a crafter. And smart businesspeople acquire help.

Most startups will immediately tell me they cannot afford to hire someone. This is faulty thinking. As an entrepreneur, you'd best avoid forecasting your situations with notions of not being able to do something.

In order to acquire help, you must first understand scalability.

IS YOUR SOAP AND SKINCARE BUSINESS SCALABLE?

If your business is based on the particular skills and talents of just you, the owner, then scaling will be difficult. If you continue to be the only producer of goods for your business, your company will only grow within the limits of your capability and stamina. There is a ceiling to how much you can produce and sell. A truly scalable soap and skincare business is one that keeps low marginal costs while increasing revenue. Moreover, I strongly believe that a truly successful soap and skincare business is one that, over time, works efficiently with less involvement from you, the business owner. Read that again. Depending on where you are on your business journey, that last sentence might freak you out a bit, but keep reading.

I had a very hard time giving up my own producing responsibilities and hiring someone to make my soap and products. I had worked hard for years producing my products and I wasn't ready to give them up, even though I needed to. I was spread too thin and on the verge of collapse before I finally started to look into hiring someone to make soap for me. Before I hired my first soapmaker employee, I knew I had to look strongly at the numbers. I, perhaps like yourself, just assumed that I couldn't afford to hire someone. But, I was wrong. There was enough in the margins to allocate some to an employee.

Let's look at a simple, watered-down example of how we can go about finding enough money in the margin to hire someone:

A start-up company makes and sells a variety of bar soaps. Its average cost in raw materials is $1.00. Each bar sells for $7.50. Each sale generates a $6.50 gross profit margin.

The company sells an average of 500 bars per month, which is $3,750 in total sales, $3,250 in gross profit (Total Sales – Raw Materials = Gross Profit)

In addition to the cost of raw materials, here is a short list (keep reading for a longer list!) of other expenses this particular company assumes in a month:

- → Owner Salary $1,000
- → Rent $1,000
- → Charitable Proceeds (1%) $37.50
- → Utilities $150
- → Website Marketing Firm $50
- → Website Hosting $10
- → Office Supplies $45
- → Sales Tax (8%) $300
- → Research & Development $60
- → Insurance $50

Total Monthly Expenses: $2,702.50

Taking the $3,250 in gross profit and subtracting all other overheads, this start-up company still has $547.50 left over.

If the business owner were to hire an employee at $12 per hour, working 10 hours per week, she would be expensing $480 per month, which is still below the $547.50 left over from all other overheads.

Now that 40 hours of production time is freed up for the business owner per month, she now dedicates that time to boosting marketing, advertising, promotions and ultimately sales. She now sells 750 bars per month, instead of the 500 they had been averaging. This is a bump in gross profit margin from $3,250 to $4875 with adding only $480 in expense.

HIGHER EARNINGS WITH ONLY A SLIGHT INCREASE IN EXPENSES

In other words, she increased her company's gross profit margin by 50 percent while increasing her company's expenses by only 18 percent. Imagine if you could increase your gross profit margin by 50 percent every time you increased your necessary expenses by 18 percent! This is great scalability!

If, for example, your company earned $5,000 in gross profit in year one and expensed $4,000 of it, and you scaled up according to the above example every year, you could expect:

- → (Year 2) $7,500 gross profit, $4,720 expensed
- → (Year 3) $11,250 gross profit, $5,569.60 expensed
- → (Year 4) $16,875 gross profit, $6,572.13 expensed
- → ...and so on

Now, obviously there are more expenses in a typical soap and skincare business than the aforementioned, "watered-down" example above. Everything must be accounted for, and trust me, it adds up quickly (I delve into this subject matter deeply in my book, *Pricing Handmade Soap for Profit*). That said, you might be surprised how much your company can afford if you really get into the numbers.

No doubt you've put your heart in the realization of your soap and skin care company. But the truth is that a growing business can be overwhelming for just one person. You can't control everything and be everywhere. You just can't. At least, not if you want to really grow your company. Making your business scalable ultimately means that you will become less involved in its processes by transforming your role into one of high-level supervision.

Build a strong team to do what they do best. Hire the right people so you can manage the business without making every slightest decision. The best company structure is streamlined so that trusted people have leading positions. As the head of the company, you need to focus on your main strengths and confront all the landmark issues that will inevitably arise.

HOW TO HIRE SOMEONE

Before finding that perfect, soap-loving human for the job, you'll need to create a plan for paying them:

EMPLOYER IDENTIFICATION NUMBER (EIN)

In order to hire someone, you must first have a business. To have a business, you must obtain an EIN. It's free to apply for an EIN, and you should do it right after you register your business.

FIND OUT WHETHER YOU NEED STATE OR LOCAL TAX IDS

The need for a state tax ID number ties directly to whether your business must pay state taxes. Some do, some don't. Tax obligations differ at the state and local levels, so you'll need to check with your state's websites. Generally speaking, most state websites have pretty clear information on the subject matter, and help via email or phone is usually pretty good. You could even grab a phone number from your state's website, call and simply ask them how to go about hiring someone. They will point you in the right direction.

To know whether you need a state tax ID, research your state's laws regarding income taxes and employment taxes. The process to get a state tax ID number is similar to getting a federal tax ID number, but it will vary by state. You'll have to check with your state government for specific steps. Again, an email or phone call should help a great deal in this matter.

ENSURE NEW EMPLOYEES RETURN A COMPLETED W-4 FORM

Do you remember your very first paycheck? Remember trying to comprehend why the hell so much was withheld?! The purpose of Tax Form W-4 is simple; it is used by the employer to withhold the proper amount of federal income tax from an employee's paycheck. This is a requirement upon hiring someone. They must fill out a W-4.

SCHEDULE PAY PERIODS

Weekly, biweekly, or semimonthly payday schedule...the choice is yours (but check your state). It is really all about cash flow and your business. With all of my other monthly overheads coming out at once, I chose to better accomodate my cash flow by choosing a biweekly format.

ADMINISTERING PAYROLL

We ran all our accounting measures through QuickBooks, so once I started hiring, I simply utilized their payroll administration as well. Very easy. There are other payroll services on the market, some of which are very expensive. If you plan on hiring just one to two people in the near future and you are already utilizing QuickBooks, I would definitely consider them to run your payroll.

REPORT PAYROLL TAXES AS NEEDED

Paperwork, paperwork, paperwork...

A huge help for me was the IRS's Employer's Tax Guide, which provides guidance on all federal tax filing requirements that could apply to the obligations for your business.

→ https://www.irs.gov/publications/p15/index.html

EMPLOYEE OR INDEPENDENT CONTRACTOR?

I thought I was being clever when I utilized an "independent contractor" to help me in my store. Julie, a college student home for the summer, was looking for work. Before I knew what I now know about employees, I took her on as an independent contractor, even though she qualified as an employee in the most legal sense. Later that year, I got a call from my state's division of labor, asking me *exactly* what role she played as a contractor. I lied. I told the person on the phone everything she wanted to hear, none of which was what Julie actually did for me. Julie should have been an employee, as she was performing as an employee under my supervision, thus making it completely the opposite of "independent."

The state cares because they aren't getting their cut of the deal in the form of withholding tax. They will call and inquire if they sense something fishy. Do not do what I did. Play by the rules. As a small business, you can't afford the potential penalties. An independent contractor operates under a separate business name from your company (it could just be themselves, their name) and invoices for work completed. Independent contractors can sometimes qualify as employees in a legal sense. The Equal Employment Opportunity Commission created a guide for making the determination, which I strongly recommend you look through.

→ http://www.eeoc.gov/policy/docs/threshold.html#2-III-A

If your contractor is discovered to meet the legal definition of employee, you may need to pay back taxes and penalties, provide benefits, and reimburse for wages stipulated under the Fair Labor Standards Act. I got lucky. They took my word and that was that.

This shouldn't dissuade you from hiring an independent contractor if you feel the need. Typically, in our industry, a classic independent contractor relationship is a company utilizing a sales representative. But even then, you must be careful not to heavy-hand their direction in sales, as you might be breaching that fine line between an employee and a contractor.

GOOD HELP IS GREAT

As mentioned, you might be pleasantly surprised at how much money is left in your margin to hire someone. If all you could afford was 10 hours a week, that is still 520 hours in a year that allows you to focus on different aspects of your business, further your production rate with hands-on help or simply take time off to rest.

PAYING YOURSELF A SALARY

The idea of setting your own salary sounds like a dream come true to many, and it certainly can be. But, if you ask small business owners in any industry, they will tell you that it can be an arduous, complicated task to get right, mainly because there isn't really a "right" way to do it. It's a bit of a crapshoot, at least at first. Setting up a system to pay yourself as the business owner is an age-old conundrum that faces every entrepreneur planning a business. There are several different theories as how to approach this riddle; we will discuss what I would consider the two most prevalent methods:

METHOD #1: PAY YOURSELF ENOUGH TO GET BY

I believe, when starting up your company, you should pay yourself only out of your company's profits, not your total sales (also known as revenue). When you see money coming into your business, don't assume you can pay yourself a big slice of that. Before you take your cut, you must take account of all the expenses of a typical soap and skin care company. The list below, which can be found in my book, *Pricing Handmade Soap for Profit*, is at the very least a start to delving into all expenses a soap and skin care might incur. Yours might be less than this, others might be more.

Expenses:

- → Taxes (sales, payroll, etc.)
- → Employment (wage labor)
- → Rent
- → Utilities
- → Phone
- → Marketing
- → Brand Development
- → Packaging / Design
- → Booth Fees
- → Advertising Costs
- → Promotion Costs
- → Website / Internet
- → Raw Materials
- → Office Supplies
- → Tools & Equipment
- → Dues & Subscriptions
- → Insurance

- → Administrative
- → Research & Development
- → Coaching / Mentoring
- → Travel Costs
- → Shipping

If these are all the expenses your company sustains on a monthly basis, the business obviously has to cover these with sales.

Total Sales – Expenses = Profit

Remember, if you are just starting out, having the ability to take a salary from the profits of your company will ensure scalability and growth over time. If a startup soap and skin care company earns $25,000 in total sales and its expenses add up to $18,000, profit is $7,000. The owner could take a draw from this profit to ensure that as her company grows in total sales, it will still cover all expenses, as expenses will inevitably grow as total sales grow.

However...

If your business *is* still in its startup phase, you might not turn a profit during your first year or two (or three). This simply means that your expenses exceed your company's total sales. There were a few years in the beginning where my company did not turn a profit. Based on the inventory of finished goods taken at the end of the year, we had the *potential* to make a profit, but we just couldn't get enough sold before year's end to reach a point of break-even or surplus.

But, I still paid myself just a bit.

I know that completely goes against what I've just explained, but bear with me. First of all, it wasn't much, and it was certainly accounted for as an expense to the business. Second of all, there's no point in being a complete miser with your company's money if it recurrently causes you financial and emotional problems. Personal money issues are a big cause of stress, and if you're stressed, you won't make good business decisions. Undervaluing your time and the work you're doing can harm your productivity and your business, so you should pay yourself enough to live comfortably without worrying. Take out what you need to avoid causing problems for your business and your personal life, but only if your company can afford it.

Plus, it feels good to pay yourself, even if it is a very small amount. If, for example, you were to pay yourself just $25 per week for a year, you are *setting the stage* for more later. If instead, you have the attitude of, "Someday I'll pay myself," that attitude might become a commandment to your subconscious to constantly be in a state of hopeful thinking, which is one of the absolute worse things you can do to yourself as an entrepreneur.

BE SYSTEMATIC

Whether you pay yourself immediately or not, don't just dip into your business funds as needed. I've seen many startup business owners pay themselves only after a big craft show or holiday event. I can see how enticing that can be, but what about the rest of the year? These owners have a dried-up business checking account in the summer and a surplus in the holiday months, and *only then* are able to pay themselves. Even if their business grew significantly under the same cash flow circumstances, that is no way to live financially. No matter what you intend to earn yourself in salary, be systematic in how you take your draw.

If you don't have them already, a day will come when you have employees, and you will pay them systematically, the same day every week, month, etc. If you can do this with them, you can do this with your own payments. Build this into your plan right from the start, perhaps with a rising salary as your business grows. You'll get used to the amount of money you receive and won't have to worry about taking out occasional large lump sums, which might strain your business. Plus, this will also look better to your employees. Regular small payments will be more acceptable to them than random large lump-sum withdrawals from the business.

PLANNING TO GET BY

To begin planning your salary, you need to put together your own personal financial statement that lists all your living expenses, any credit cards with outstanding balances and all short-term and long-term loans. This may be one of the most difficult things you've ever had to do, as you don't want to leave anything out. You want to make sure that your income from the business will be enough to cover your personal living expenses. I strongly recommend using www.mint.com. Mint has helped Amanda and me lay the foundation for all of our financial goals. Literally every account, mortgage, car payment, student loan, stocks, IRA, etc. that we've ever had in the last few years is all in Mint. When we login in, we know exactly, in real time, how much we are worth. It is invaluable resource as an entrepreneur.

Whether you use an incredible free resource like Mint or not, you should create a personal balance sheet based off all operating expenses and goals you and yours have. If you have any outstanding debts, now is the time to focus heavily on them, as you might be viewing them all in full for the first time in one snapshot. Generally, if you can pay down any debts before going into business, you'll not only decrease the amount of income you'll require each month, but also improve your personal net worth, which is important when it comes to borrowing capital to fund your business if needed.

Once you establish each of your expenses per month, add them all together. This is the amount you will need to pay yourself in order to meet your basic living requirements. This is pretty simple stuff, as long as you stay organized. Remember to include all your expenses. You must provide yourself with complete information. After all, you will be living on this income for the foreseeable future, so you don't want to get it wrong!

Let's look at an example. Regina, who decides that she is to be a successful soap and skin care business owner, is figuring out how much to pay herself in salary, based on her personal finances. Here is the list of her *personal expenses* that come out each month:

- Mortgage: $750.00
- Car Payment: $300.00
- Credit Card: $100.00 (minimum payment)
- Student Loan: $200.00
- Health Insurance: $330.00
- Netflix: $9.00
- Gym: $20.00

→ Investment: $200.00

→ Utilities: $120.00

→ General Living: $1,200.00

This list is everything she owes per month. Her soap and skin care salary must eventually cover all of these personal living expenses in order for her to work fulltime and wholeheartedly on her business. The monthly total comes to $3,229.00. Due to unforeseen circumstances and/or emergencies, it would be smart to bump up her personal living expense number to $3,400.00 per month. Regina now knows that eventually she will need to take a salary of $3,400 per month to continue her current lifestyle, and perhaps increase this as her business grows. This comes to an annual salary of $40,800.

Now, will Regina be able to rake in that much in her first year? Probably not. And this, more than anything else, is why starting a business is so damned hard. Most entrepreneurs who start businesses make serious financial sacrifices while also taking on serious financial risk. If it were easy, everyone would have their own business. It's not easy. Regina has to make a solid plan that gets her business to the point of affording her steady payments totaling at least $40,800 in one calendar year. If Regina can work into this salary over the course of a few years, she will be on the right track. If her business isn't doing well over the first few years, she might be in real financial trouble.

Your business will not be fruitful unless you establish clear financial goals, with your own personal livelihood in mind. If you are creating a soap and skin care company as a side thing, without needing to draw a salary, no worries. But, if you eventually intend to pivot away from whatever your main financial earnings are right now into being a successful business owner, you'll need to establish a salary. This method is how I wiggled my way into a financial living. I simply did the numbers, as numbers don't lie (as long as they are all in front of you!), and came up with an owner draw that would cover my personal financial livelihood that could eventually come from my company's checking account on a systematic basis.

METHOD #2: PAY YOURSELF WHAT YOU ARE WORTH

This method is a bit tougher to conceptualize. The first method allows for you to basically squirm your way into a salary as time goes on and your business grows. This method requires a lot of planning, but don't shy away from it. As long as you build your salary into your company's future plans, you will have an accurate portrayal of how much in total sales your company will need to generate (your revenue goals). Thus, by paying yourself *what you are worth*, you aren't painting an artificial portrait of your business that will change once you reach a successful, functioning rate of growth. This method is all about some simple mathematics.

So, how much do you feel you are worth? This is a very subjective question. Let's start by looking at your current circumstance. For example, do you work a job right now? Are you on salary or an hourly wage? What is it? How much do you get paid in one year in your current position? Whatever the number, that is what your market worth is at this point in time (whether you like it or not). I believe this is what you want to make *at a minimum* going into business for yourself. But market worth isn't basic worth. There is a difference. Basic worth is your market worth plus a percentage increase based on three to four times the rate of inflation. Breathe. Allow me to explain.

Remember, market worth is a minimum, a starting point. What you are *currently* making in your job now is your financial floor. It doesn't take into consideration the increased responsibilities of running a business and your value to the business as its owner. With these factors taken into consideration, your basic worth is determined using the following equation:

(MW (12) [1 (I (4) = BW

In this equation, market worth (MW) is your total annual pay minus any bonuses or overtime. Again, this is the floor. This is the bare bones of what you make from your current job, or a job you've had in the past. Divide the annual market worth by 12 to get a monthly amount. Then multiply this by the inflation percentage (I), and then multiply that by four.

For example, let's say you are currently earning $20 per hour at your current job, and you work 40 hours per week. At $20 per hour, your annual pay would be $41,600 (20 x 40 hours = 800 x 52 weeks = 41,600). Your annual pay of $41,600 would then be divided by 12, resulting in a monthly income of $3,466. Let's say the annual rate of inflation is 4 percent. You would then multiply four by four, (4% x 4, per the equation above), which gives you 16. This is the percentage which you will add to your current monthly income – 16 percent. When we incorporate this back into your current salary, (41,600 x 0.16 = 6,656 + 41,600 = $48,256), you are now worth $48,256 on an annual basis.

Please keep in mind that this is merely a recommended model to use when determining what you will pay yourself during the period of startup. You don't have to do this at all, but it gives you a starting point. As opposed to paying yourself enough to get by, seen in method one, this method gives you a slightly more accurate (and justified) salary number for you to shoot for. There isn't a right or wrong between the two methods. You can use either, or some other system. The idea is to provide you with a realistic figure that's fair and equitable to your current financial lifestyle, to which you can increase later as your business grows.

If you currently have a job that affords you a lifestyle you enjoy, at the very minimum this should be your ideal salary when starting your business.

LEGAL AND TAX CONSIDERATIONS

How much you can pay yourself, and when, might be restricted by the legal structure of your business. Many people fail to realize that when you're self-employed, the legal form under which you operate your business directly affects the way the IRS views your tax status and, therefore, will have some bearing on how you pay yourself.

SOLE PROPRIETORSHIP

The easiest way to get into business is as a sole proprietor. A sole proprietor doesn't have partners to worry about, or a corporate identity to hide behind. As a sole proprietor, the buck stops at your desk and nobody else's. As sole proprietors, you're basically free to pay yourself whatever and whenever you like. That's partly because you're not accountable to shareholders or stockholders. But, if you get tagged with a lawsuit, you face the liability. This is the unfortunate legal side to a sole proprietorship. On the other hand, if your company does well, you reap the profits. Under a sole proprietorship, profits from the business and your personal income are treated the same by the IRS. There is no distinction. This is the great advantage to the income and tax side of a sole proprietorship.

PARTNERSHIP

A partnership is totally different from sole proprietorship in terms of operations, but from the point of view of the IRS, they are practically the same. Any profit generated through a partnership is treated as personal income. Unlike sole proprietors completing Schedule C of Form 1040, partnerships must file Form 1065, U.S. Partnership Return of Income. This lists all expenses that can be directed against income to arrive at the taxable income generated from your business. A Schedule K-1 should be sent to each partner to help them report their share of the income on Form 1040.

At Prairie Soap Company, our legal structure was a multi-member limited liability company (LLC) partnership. Because we were not incorporated, as managing members—myself, my brother and my mother—could basically pay ourselves whenever we wanted, and however much we wanted. We did this for a time, and then eventually became more systematic about our payment structure. When we hired employees, we ran payroll for them, but we, the managing members, were still able to pay ourselves when we wanted and whatever we wanted. That said, we acted as if we were also on the payroll, just like our employees, thus cutting ourselves a check every week for the same amount.

CORPORATION

If your business is organized as a corporation, you will get paid a salary like other employees. Any profit the business makes will accrue to the corporation, not to you personally. At the end of the year, you must file a corporate income tax return. The salary you receive from the corporation is, of course, reported as your own personal income. As the CEO of a corporation, you'll be able to plan your salary with an eye toward tax rates. Keep in mind there are S-Corporations and C-Corporations, which are taxed differently, so do your homework.

PLANNING FOR GROWTH

At this point in the book, I hope you can see the true power of a plan. Shooting from the hip can only get you so far before someone eventually guns you down. In the entrepreneurial world, that someone is usually yourself. Lack of foresight and planning your financial numbers, will inevitably lead to poor salaries, the inability to hire someone (which inhibits growth) and lack of scalability. Remember, over time, your company needs to scale up production and profit while keeping expenses as low as possible (knowing that they *will* rise with more revenue). The profit margins of your company will determine your salary and ability to hire.

Let's take another look at the list of typical expenses in a soap and skin care company:
- → Taxes (sales, payroll, etc.)
- → Employment (wage labor)
- → Rent
- → Utilities

- → Phone
- → Marketing
- → Brand Development
- → Packaging / Design
- → Booth Fees
- → Advertising Costs
- → Promotion Costs
- → Website / Internet
- → Raw Materials
- → Office Supplies
- → Tools & Equipment
- → Dues & Subscriptions
- → Insurance
- → Administrative
- → Research & Development
- → Coaching / Mentoring
- → Travel Costs
- → Shipping
- → **Salary**

Now let's run some example numbers. If this is everything a soap and skin care company incurs as expenses, we can fill in some monthly numbers (keep in mind that some of these are monthly averages):

→ Taxes (sales, payroll, etc.)	$300
→ Employment (wage labor)	$500
→ Rent	$700
→ Utilities	$150
→ Phone	$50
→ Marketing	$100

→	Brand Development	$100
→	Advertising Costs	$100
→	Promotion Costs	$50
→	Website / Internet	$40
→	Raw Materials	$2,000
→	Office Supplies	$30
→	Tools & Equipment	$10
→	Dues & Subscriptions	$10
→	Insurance	$50
→	Administrative	$50
→	Research & Development	$20
→	Coaching / Mentoring	$85
→	Travel Costs	$10
→	Shipping	$250
→	**Salary**	**$2,500**

The sum total of all these expenses comes to $7,105 in one month. This simply means that the business needs to sell $7,105 per month to break even, and anything over that would be seen as a positive net margin.

It's as simple as making a plan, putting it down on paper and then beginning the execution of the plan. Numbers don't lie. Take this list of typical expenses and start making your own projections. Maybe you don't have to pay for rent right now, as you work from home. That would be a huge cost-saver to get your company moving in the right direction. Or, maybe you don't yet have employees, which saves on both hourly wage and payroll and administrative fees. This is a huge cost-saver to get your company moving. Whatever your current position is, make realistic projections of all the expenses your company will incur every month and then make a sales plan (goals) to cover or exceed the summed expenses.

Only when you do this, will you find the money to provide yourself a healthy salary and the ability to hire someone.

CHAPTER 10:

CREATING HYPE

Nearly 75 percent of startups fail within the first three years. The classic saying, "prior planning prevents poor performance" applies directly to a startup. It could not be more relevant. There needs to be an established audience presence beforehand to achieve this. It is crucial to look at the big picture and how you can build up excitement that will grow your business.

Marketing is the process of instructing potential customers why they should choose your soap and skin care products over another company's. If you are not doing that, you are not marketing. It really is that simple. Now, most people can create a few ideas on paper that direct potential customers to their awesome products; but you have to do a bit more than that by bringing your own identity into the fold, your company's own voice, to instruct with importance and emphasis. The key is creating the *right* marketing method for your specific company and defining the *right* marketing message to educate and influence your consumers.

Companies make the mistake of thinking that marketing is just "one" thing ("I have to get my marketing done today"), but marketing is *everything* your potential customer might encounter when it comes to your business – advertising, what they hear, the customer service that they receive, the follow-up care that you provide. Everything.

MARKETING VS. ADVERTISING:

WHAT'S THE DIFFERENCE?

Marketing is often confused with advertising and sales, but it is important to know the key differences.

Advertising: The paid, public, non-personal announcement of a persuasive message by an identified sponsor; the non-personal presentation or promotion by a firm of its products to its existing and potential customers.

Marketing: The systematic planning, implementation, and control of a *mix* of business activities intended to bring together buyers and sellers for the mutually advantageous exchange or transfer of products.

Even after reading these definitions, it might still be a bit confusing, so let's go into each with a bit more depth.

ADVERTISING

I like to think of advertising as just a *single component* of the entire marketing process. Advertising is the part that involves getting the word out concerning your soap and skin care business and your products, which requires payment. It involves the process of developing strategies such as ad placement, frequency, etc. Thus, advertising includes the placement of an ad in such mediums as newspapers, direct mail, billboards, television, radio, and of course the Internet.

Generally speaking, advertising is the largest expense of all marketing plans. The best way to distinguish between advertising and marketing is to think of marketing as a pie, and inside that pie you have slices of advertising, market research, media planning, public relations, product pricing, distribution, customer support, sales strategy, and community involvement. Advertising equals only *one* piece of the pie in the strategy, albeit an incredibly important one and often under-utilized in the cottage, artisan industry.

Everyone knows Coca-Cola. They are the single-most recognized brand in the world. The freaking world! Yet they constantly advertise. Their advertising budget is beyond understanding! Think about this. Even though they are doing just fine, they *still* advertise in all media platforms imaginable. Why? Because it is that important!

MARKETING

Marketing is a step-by-step process that begins with a solid mission and set of vision and values. This foundation then acts as a guiding theme and identity which helps you identify target customers who are interested in your soap and skin care products. Once you determine who your target audience is, your marketing plan will then help you map out a strategy to best position your products. And after these strategies and tactics are developed, you will *then* be ready to focus on an advertising strategy that will help you explain, teach and promote your products to different audiences in as many media platforms as possible – from film, television, newspapers and magazines, the Internet, or to any other mediums you can think of.

Okay, now that you know the difference between marketing and advertising, and that advertising is a piece of the marketing pie, let's look at the 10,000-foot view of marketing your soap and skin care company.

FOUR P'S OF MARKETING:

#1 PRODUCTS

You probably already have your products made and ready to sell. Or, you might have an idea for a set of products that you would like to take to market. And to both, I say, great!

But I would encourage you to really think about your current product line. Begin a fun procedure called the "ideation stage," where you can really conceive a unique product. There is so much soap to be found everywhere. Etsy is flooded with soap. Instagram is full of beautifully-presented soaps. Niche stores, boutiques, department stores, specialty shops, even vending machines – everyone is selling soap.

So, what makes *your* soap unique? And sorry to say this, but your ingredients only go so far. How *else* can you captivate your audience with your products beyond the utility of their use and the list of ingredients? Remember the Absolut Vodka example. They utilized marketing aesthetics to capture a unique audience.

What are you doing to capture a unique audience with your products? What's your style? Your scents? Your sizes? Your packaging design? And, by the way, if you think that "natural" and "eco-friendly" are enough to make your company stand out these days, you're delusional. Every other soap company is natural or eco-friendly. That might have worked 10 years ago, but not today.

#2 PRICE

Soap and skin care companies must know the optimal price to sell their products to achieve maximum return. One way to determine price is to set it at a level comparable to competitors, but *only* if the company can recover all associated product expenses and still make a profit (see my book, *Selling Handmade Soap for Profit*). Customers will pay only so much for products. After you've established who your company is (your identity), found who will purchase (your customer), and then made sure all expenses will be covered (your margin), you can price your products appropriately. A certain price can be marketed to a certain person through aesthetics and voice.

#3 PROMOTION

Promotion pertains to brochures, ads, and information that companies use to generate interest in their products. This is also an often-under-utilized action in the cottage, artisan industry. Furthermore, when I see a set of promotional materials from an artisan start-up, it often lacks cohesion.

#4 PLACE

Place in marketing nomenclature is the distribution. Wholesale? Direct retail via store? Online retail? Tradeshows? Each distribution channel utilized might need a slightly different marketing effort. All distribution decisions are part of the overall marketing process.

EASY MARKETING IDEAS

Now that we've discussed some of the larger concepts of marketing, let's stroll through some actionable ideas to get you moving in the right direction with your marketing efforts. Beyond what you've already discovered in this book, such as branding, aesthetics, customer demographics and the importance of creating a strong voice through a mission, vision and set of values, let's see what else we can come up with.

CONDUCT A FOCUS GROUP

Before you think to yourself that your company is too small and insignificant to conduct a focus group, please keep reading. A focus group is very simple. It involves having potential purchasers come together to experience something, whether it be your actual products, or walking them through an email marketing campaign to see how easy or confusing it is. Each member of the group then shares his/her opinions, criticisms and other feedback about the experience by answering the same set of questions posed by an interviewer; in your case, probably you or a team member. A focus group can be an incredibly effective way for small businesses to conduct their very own market research as part of the creation of their marketing plan.

A focus group may be an appropriate market research activity for your business in these situations:

- → You are in the process of developing a cool, new skin care product and want input during the development phase.
- → You are revamping your branding approach and want to get an idea of which aesthetics may be more effective and appealing.
- → You are simply clueless about how your website looks to other people, because you've looked at it so much you might be blind to it.
- → You are interested in discovering new ideas, formats and approaches that you haven't thought of yourself.
- → You want to find out about the motivation behind a specific action or inaction you are thinking of taking within your business.
- → There is a communication gap between your business and your target market.

As you can see, focus groups can be a unique way to get into the heads of your target market and get feedback they wouldn't normally provide, at least not to your face! Whether they respond to a questionnaire on paper or vocally to you, people may be more candid in their responses because they appreciate what you are trying to do. Plus, a group setting can make participants more willing to share their insight, as they won't feel like they will get lambasted by giving a critique. If you conduct a focus group in person, you can learn from actions, body language and other nonverbal communication, which can be invaluable. Most importantly, you can learn about the *perception* people have about you, your business and/or your products. And perception is everything.

There are seemingly thousands of market-research firms that will conduct a focus group on your company's behalf. They can be quite expensive, but certainly effective. That said, you can conduct your own focus group by thinking outside the box.

Just after we received our company's soap box samples, fully equipped with everything needed to create a larger wholesale distribution, we conducted a focus group to see what we might be missing in the design and overall aesthetic of our packaging before we went ahead with ordering 10,000 of them.

I asked a handful of friends and family members to bring one or two friends that I did not know, who were also to bring one or two friends who I did not know, over for a get-together for some party favors and spirits, knowing that they would be my focus group. Because of the degrees of mandated separation, I was ensuring more objectivity in their responses, as opposed to just having friends and/or family over. The whole experience was quite entertaining, as there were many people in one house who didn't actually know one another. With everyone knowing the goal of the party being to objectively discuss our products and their packaging, the atmosphere was fun and light.

Everything about our business was eventually discussed. Everything. Though the goal was to garner feedback from our packaging, we deliberated on many different aspects of our business, which ultimately propelled our company into its eventual success. The way in which we conducted our focus group was fun, creative and absolutely mind-opening to some actionable ideas that I honestly never thought of. Be creative and think outside the box to get some truly excellent feedback about any and all aspects of your business. Just don't take criticism personally and be open to suggestions.

MARKETING MATERIALS AND MEDIA

If your business cards suck and don't represent your mission, vision and values, or don't have the right fonts or color palette, update them. If you need, pay someone to design quality business cards.

Do the same for flyers and brochures.

If your website sucks, change it. Update it. You can't afford to have a poorly designed, unaesthetic website. In today's world, your website is a huge part of your identity, so get it right. Furthermore, websites should never be static. You must constantly change the banners to indicate sales and deals, create opt-in newsletter sign-ups and recurrently post written blogs and videos to keep things fresh.

REGISTER FOR A CONFERENCE OR TRADESHOW

Whether the Alabama Soap & Candle Meeting, the Lone Star Soap & Toiletries Seminar or the Handcrafted Soap & Cosmetic Guild's annual conference (there are many more), be a part of one to garner ideas and bump shoulders with people who might know more than you.

As far as direct business to business operations, tradeshows are a fantastic way to market your products to likeminded companies who might be interested in purchasing from you. Wholesale and trade shows are typically shows that are not open to the general public, but to buyers who will come and place orders for your product. At most trade shows, you set up a booth with samples of your products. Buyers will write orders, which you will ship at a later date. (There are a few shows that are cash and carry in which buyers purchase your product onsite to take back to their stores. I would recommend you start with a traditional order-writing show since it requires less inventory up front.)

There is a plethora of wholesale tradeshows across the country every year. Though there are many websites dedicated to listing wholesale tradeshows, a good place to start is www.wholesalecentral.com.

Showing well at a wholesale tradeshow can literally put your business on the map for years to come. Some shows cost a serious penny, but the return on investment could serve to be the catalyst for your company's success moving forward.

DIRECT MAIL CAMPAIGN

Though it may seem archaic to market your company through direct mail these days, it is still an effective way to showcase your business, as long as you include a clear and enticing call to action on every direct mail piece you send out. Among others, Staples (www.staples.com) has an easy, 3-step process to send out direct mail. You can search by zip code, postal route, or even demographics with their "point and click" mapping tool, or upload your own list to get started. Then, upload your design (the actual flyer, postcard, etc.), or work with one of their designers to complete a piece. Once you place your order, they handle everything else. This is an effective method, as not only can you send out your marketing messages to specific demographics, but you can see what return you get on the investment over time.

ADVERTISE!

- Advertise on your local radio stations. At the very least, call and get an idea of the cost and work that into your budget.
- If you have a prominence on shopping locally and you're in a bigger city, advertise on a billboard in a busy area. Call and get an idea of the cost and work that into your budget!
- Use stickers and/or magnets and light up your car with them! Pass them around town, or put them in your direct mailers.
- Take out an ad in your local newspaper. Better yet, call the paper to see if they will run a fun story on your enterprising business!
- Advertise on a local cable television station. Call and get an idea of the cost and work that into your budget. Yes, it will be expensive, but don't just say, "no" to the idea forever! Find out more information and then make a plan!
- Advertise on social media.
- Buy advertising space on prominent, high-traffic websites.
- Make tee-shirts with your logo and website on them. People love swag!

START A BLOG

Have a website? Start a blog on your site! Business blogging is a marketing tactic that uses blogging to get your business more online visibility. A business blog is a marketing channel (just like social media, direct mail, email marketing, etc.) that helps support business growth.

More than anything else, blogging drives traffic to your site. Instead of (or in addition to) spending lots of money on search engine optimization (SEO) tools, by simply blogging on a recurrent basis, search engines

(Google, Yahoo, etc.) will "see" your site as important and thus drive you further to the top of the search list.

Think about how many pages are on your website. Probably not a ton, right? And think about how often you update those pages. Probably not that often, right? Well, blogging helps solve both of those problems.

Every time you write a blog post, it's one more indexed page on your website, which means it's one more opportunity for you to show up in search engines and drive traffic to your website. Blogging also helps you get discovered via social media. Every time you write a blog post, you're creating content that people can share on social networks, which helps expose your business to a new audience that may not yet know you.

Blog content also helps keep your social media presence going. Instead of constantly having to come up with new original content for social media (or hiring someone to do it), your blog can serve as that repository of content. You're strengthening your social reach with blog content and driving new website visitors to your blog via your social channels.

So, let's say you start blogging regularly, and traffic picks up. Now you have a golden opportunity to convert that traffic into leads. Just like every blog post you write is another indexed page for search engines to find you and see you as important, each post is a new opportunity to generate new leads, as long as you create a call-to-action on every blog post.

Let's say you make a new whipped body butter and scent it with Lavender essential oil. You then write a blog post about the aromatherapeutic benefits of Lavender, how it is harvested, and where your Lavender (used in your whipped body butter) came from in this big world. Then, at the bottom, you have a call-to-action that says, "Use coupon code 'LoveLav' for 20 percent your entire order of whipped body butter!" This entire sentence is a link that sends the onlooker to the new whipped body butter product page on your site.

This is what we call a sales funnel.

You have created interesting, free content with a call-to-action that is relative to the conversation. The call-to-action "funnels" customers directly to an easy click to add to cart. This is just one example of a call-to-action. What if you did this every week? That is 52 different calls-to-action in a year, resulting in a very large potential readership to be converted to customers.

As a long-term approach to online marketing, business blogging sets you up as an authority figure on whatever it is you are selling. You can be seen as an industry mogul by writing effective blog posts, creating video content, etc. All of this work will ultimately establish you as an authority in the eyes of consumers. This is a vital piece of marketing in the artisan world.

CREATE A GROUPON

I love Groupon! I am repeatedly purchasing deals from Groupon, and we utilized this easy marketing service in my company all the time. It definitely pays off, as Groupon has a serious cult-following.

CREATE A YOUTUBE CHANNEL

If you're only using YouTube as a place to watch funny cat videos or find the latest underground band, you're missing out on its benefits as a powerful business tool to enhance your brand and strengthen your social outreach. The number one way people find new businesses is through

YouTube. Behind Google, YouTube is the second-largest search engine in the world.

Having a branded channel on YouTube allows you to customize the appearance of your page, providing a more consistent look and feel from the website to the channel by incorporating banners and background images. You'll be able to create additional tabs for custom content sections. And, a branded channel also increases opportunities for optimization efforts which can help your company become more visible online.

Remember, YouTube is the second largest search engine next to Google. The tagging feature on YouTube allows you to tag keywords for each video, and these tags communicate to the search engines the subjects of your videos. YouTube also offers its own Analytics so you can monitor visits, best performing videos, etc. Plus, YouTube integrates easily with other social media platforms like Facebook, Google+, Twitter, Pinterest, and Tumblr. The links to these channels are included in the brand banner so users can easily access additional content.

CREATE AN EMAIL OPT-IN ON YOUR WEBSITE

This is another great funneling technique. Email marketing is gaining more and more traction in the business world. As a consumer, I utilize the powerful marketing effects of emailing all the time. I am constantly looking at deals from Groupon, GNC and a host of other companies to which I have signed up for their email newsletter. I am being funneled all the time, and I love it because it is convenient for me.

An opt-in is a form of consent given by web users, acknowledging interest in a product or service and authorizing a third party to contact them with further information. "Opting in" generally refers to email communication and is often used in ecommerce for permission to send newsletters, product sales, and other marketing material to customers. Opt-in forms can be presented to customers and visitors in a variety of ways: pop-up forms on the homepage or product pages, dedicated landing pages, and built-in widgets across an ecommerce website.

Collecting emails is definitely something you should be doing, especially if you really want to create a strong online retail revenue stream. Being consistent with your branding is so important for building credibility. You want to give people the feeling that you take your website seriously and your opt-in offer is a big part of that. Having a clearly designed opt-in will not only help readers understand what you do, but also make them feel more comfortable giving you their personal contact information.

Your opt-in form is one of the most important elements on your website (or at least your homepage). What good is it if someone comes to your website and then leaves without ever giving you a way to contact them? Everyone has a short attention span so if you don't grab your visitors during those critical first moments, well you just missed out. Not only does your opt-in form have to get noticed, it also has to be something that your audience actually wants. You want your messaging to resonate so your audience can't wait to join your list. Be impactful and results-focused. Tell visitors what benefits they'll get out of signing up.

OFFER A FREE DOWNLOAD OR FREE GIFT

What if, on your email opt-in mechanism, you offer a free pdf download with "Top 10 Benefits to Using Lavender in Your Home." So, they sign up to find in their inbox a free pdf download. They read the single-page download, and then find at the bottom a call-to-action in the form of a coupon code, which funnels them back to your website for a purchase opportunity. See how that works? This technique is called "lead generation." I recommend utilizing the services of Leadpages (www.leadpages.net) to create a nicely branded email opt-in.

BE CONSISTENT WITH YOUR EMAIL NEWSLETTERS

What if, over time, you generate an email list of 5,000 people? And what if you proposed a sale or promotion every two weeks via an email newsletter? What if your email list had an industry-average open rate of about 30 percent? What if 20 percent of those who open the email and read through it are funneled to your site and purchase? What if the average purchase rate is $25?

That is $7,500 in total sales every two weeks, which equals $195,000 in total sales for the year. And this is just from *one* marketing campaign performed every two weeks (26 times in a year).

Do this. You will start your email list with one person. Then two. Then ten, and so on. Build your list into the thousands and then simply create effective calls-to-action on each and every newsletter you send out.

Mail Chimp (www.mailchimp.com), Constant Contact (www.constantcontact.com), and Aweber (www.aweber.com) are three of the best companies for garnering emails and sending out effective campaigns.

SEND OUT CUSTOMER SATISFACTION SURVEYS

Surveying your customers regularly and in a variety of ways is a critical part of running a successful soap and skin care business. Surveys measure satisfaction, or dissatisfaction, with your offerings, determine critical needs and offer an opportunity to effectively communicate and build truly personal relationships with your customers. And when you take both praise and criticism to heart in order to fulfill the true needs of these customers, you build invaluable loyalty that can create buzz around your business and bring in enthusiastic, highly qualified referrals (word of mouth).

The most enlightening customer feedback often comes from just picking up the phone and having direct contact with customers. This could be done with your wholesale customers, or simply with your online retail customers, as you will have their contact information via their payment method. Your survey feedback is worthless if you don't take action on it. You need to put plans in place to resolve issues revealed by surveys and always reconnect with customers that express dissatisfaction.

You will be amazed at what this does for your business. Even if you don't conduct a formal survey, you can still call on people to seek their opinion on your business. I would often email or call customers, whether they came in the store or purchased online just to say hello and to thank them for their purchase. I would ask if our products met their expectations and seek their opinion on the utility of our products.

This simple act made them feel so good. People just don't do this anymore, but you can. Be familiar, personal and open with how you are, and your customers will reciprocate. And, this is the easiest way to get referrals. People will go out of their way to get you more customers if you show kindness and a willingness to listen.

CHARITY

Whether through applied action or monetarily, giving a piece of your company to the community is a great way to market your business. I can't really see a downside to doing this. Everyone wins.

After we opened the doors to our store, we really wanted to create a strong sense of belonging with our community. That spring, on Earth Day, we had a huge party in our store. We advertised locally, telling everyone to come out, bring their kids and have a beer and snacks on us. We hired a personal masseuse who set up in our production room, providing 10-minute massages to anyone who wanted one. We ran specials all day long. We had a special play-area set up for kids, and my Dad would color and draw with them as their parents dawdled around the store, drinking beer and meeting new friends. We gave a percentage to the Earth Day Network, which was sizeable and worth it for everyone.

Later that year, I asked my neighboring store owners or managers (we were in the middle of a large shopping center filled with big box chain stores) if they would pick a representative from their store as a volunteer to help pick up trash in our local parks. We had volunteers from Macy's, JC Penney, Joseph A Banks, Finish Line and plenty more all come out to pick up trash at a local park. This garnered the attention of the town paper, which came out and ran a story on it. The reporter kept asking the crew whose idea this was, to all come together from different businesses to do this, and everyone pointed at me. So, I was interviewed about it, and our business saw a huge uptick in patrons and sales for many following months.

What can you do to create a shared sense of belonging? How can you incorporate charitable action or giving and then get credited for it in a marketable way?

SPONSOR A LOCAL SPORTS TEAM

From Pop-Warner to professional, sponsoring a team can really put your business on the map.

HOLIDAY THANK-YOU GIFTS

For your top 10 to 20 customers, whether online or wholesale, send them a beautiful gift package. These types of gestures have immense marketing value. Do the same with birthdays.

HIRE A PROFESSIONAL

You can't not engage in marketing. If all of this marketing-scheming you are reading scares you, or you just don't want to do it, you company still needs it. So, hire someone. Hire a copywriter to write your content. Hire a marketing consultant. I do both of these things, and I'd be happy to help if you need. From life coaching to branding and marketing development, I charge an hourly fee to create needed content for companies, so long as they are serious about their business. Or, you might be able to hire someone locally, to have sit-down consultations when needed. The point is, this stuff is a requirement to your success, so if you can't do it, you must delegate it.

Some of these ideas are easier to implement than others, but they are all doable. If you were to partake in just a few of these ideas, your business will be better for it.

SETTING UP A MARKETING CALENDAR

Whether you hire someone or not, you must still take the reins of your marketing efforts, and do so from a long-term perspective. At the very least, one year.

By fall at the latest, of whatever year it is, be looking at your marketing efforts for the *following* year. Having a plan in place to market your company before the year even starts is one of the most important things you can do for your business and your own sanity. Let's look at some examples of how you can do this now, before the following year starts. Let's say it is October 1, and you sit down to plan for next year's marketing efforts:

Blog posts:

You've decided you want to blog on your website. You want to be consistent, so you decide on one post per week. You want to post with a mix of media, both written and visual, so you decide on both the written word and videos as your blog post mediums of choice.

You know there are 52 weeks in a year, so you come up with 52 blog post ideas. Of these 52 ideas, you decide that 32 will be written and 20 will be video. Now that you have all of your ideas down, get out your calendar for next year and start placing each idea in the appropriate time of year.

Then, start writing and recording. Chunk down your writing ideas into two written, fully edited blog posts per day, which is 10 in a week (five working days). This only takes you three weeks and two days to complete. Meanwhile, you also chunk down your video ideas into three per day. You see, there is nothing wrong with completing all of your videos in this way. The more you can chunk in one day, the better! Since you only need 20, you are finished in just one week.

Now you have all of your blog post content ready to go before the year even starts.

Email newsletter campaigns:

You've decided that you are going to send out three email campaigns per month, with each having a call-to-action. This is just 36 email campaigns to compile, so you start your list. You begin thinking about all of the ways in which you can tie in the year, the holidays, seasons, etc. to garner some attention with your newsletters:

- → January Campaign #1: *"Our New Year's Day event will be extended for one week! Come over to mywebsite.com and use the coupon code, 'newyear' to receive 15 percent off your entire purchase!"*
- → January Campaign #2: *"Mothers, it is time to treat yourself!...you must be tired of buying and wrapping presents; preparing for all the family for the holidays; cooking and constantly cleaning up after friends and family; putting everyone before yourself. Well, it's a new year! It is time to take care of YOU. Jump over to mywebsite.com and use the coupon code, "mytime" and get 20 percent off..."*
- → January Campaign #3: *"It's dry skin month! We are still in the thick of winter and it isn't going away anytime soon. Pay attention to dry skin with our lemon-scented whipped shea butter (big product picture of shea butter that links to the product on your site)!"*

And so on.

Prepare each month this way and you have all 36 email marketing campaigns ready to go!

You see, this was just *two* different marketing efforts (One being 52 blog posts and the second being 36 email campaigns) that are not only easy to implement, but wildly effective in the online realm. What if, in addition, you added a "soap of the month" campaign, to which you dedicated two more email newsletters per month/soap? Now you are at five email campaigns per month, along with one blog/video post per week. Do you see how easy this becomes with some simple planning?

Take the time to sit down and plan the year in advance. You'll be amazed at the ideas you can come up with, and then quickly start implementing. Plus, planning out all of your marketing events will actually dictate your production/manufacturing. Your entire production calendar can be based on marketing events. What I see most often in our industry is the opposite of this, in which a maker will create a bunch of product and then try to find a marketable approach to getting rid of it. I would advise to first create an effective marketing plan and then base your production plans from it. Another great resource for implementing new and easy ideas is Amanda's eBook, *Marketing Your Handcrafted Soap, Candle or Cosmetics Business* (http://www.lovinsoap.com/shop/marketing-handcrafted-soap-candle-cosmetics-business-ebook/).

CONCLUSION

I firmly believe that branding your business is, and should be, a lot of fun. Creating a persona out of thin air and materializing it into existence through the creation of a business is a truly amazing undertaking, albeit a time-consuming and mentally strenuous one. I hope that you've seen in this book that your product-making, while important, is really a marginal component to your overall success. Your products must be good, yes. And if they aren't quite yet, you will get there through research, trial and error. But brand-building a soap and skin care company into this world should really be taking the lion's share of your everyday focus.

You can achieve big things with your soap and skin care business, as long as you take the mental handcuffs off your dreams. It's okay to dream big. It's okay to develop a knowing that you will achieve whatever it is you write down on paper, even if it hasn't yet shown up. This is the essence of entrepreneurialism.

I know I was a bit hard on you in the second chapter, Money Mindset, but I felt the need to set the tone early. It's okay to love money and to want more of it. If you never get your mind and emotions wrapped around this, you probably aren't cut out for giving this your all, which is okay if that suits your sensibilities. But, if you really want to make a living from a beautiful business that you form from your endless creativity, there is a built-in requirement – a good relationship with money. I implore you to develop this within yourself, and if you have to start with forgiveness, whether self or someone else, by all means, do so.

Part of making the decision to be successful and then following through with massive action is listening to the right people and leaving the wrong people behind. I've blatantly had to stop being around some friends I've known for almost three decades, simply because they projected a mindset of lack, doubt, fear and criticism. They weren't aiding me in my quest to be my best self, run my best company and serve the most people possible. They didn't fit into that scheme, so I had to move on. I know that may sound harsh, but you are the accumulation of the people you spend the most time with, so make sure they are wildly successful and creative. If you don't' have any wildly successful and creative people in your life, hire a coach.

Without a mission, your company will not succeed on a large enough level to compensate yourself appropriately. Your company must have a north star. You must engage in a sense of duty that goes far beyond making products. Your mission, vision and set of values comprise the DNA of your business. Don't take this lightly.

This book was written in large part to accentuate the need for originality and style in our industry. Be you. Come original in every single component of your business, from the name, to the logo, your fonts, your websites, products, product names, product packaging, photography, *everything*. Put your company spin on every component of your business – some "thing" that can only be portrayed through your enduring originality and no one else's. Style matters. Be wildly innovative in your approach.

Everything is in a name. As I write this, we are about to have a baby. We won't know the gender until the big day, so we have a short list of names picked out for either gender. The process we took to pick out our baby's name was fun. It was creative. It harked back to our most cherished moments as humans. It brought in family backgrounds and storied images of how our ancestors got their names. It made us think in such a vast measure – something I did not expect when the process started.

Naming your company and your products should be fun, creative and meaningful.

Your customer is your business. Your products are not. Yes, your products certainly play a role, but your customers put food on your table. You must know who they are. Do your research. Reread this book and implement some actionable steps to get to know who you are targeting. You can't please everyone. If you try, you will fail. Find out who will fall in love with your brand, and then find their friends, and then find their friends, and then find their friends…

You create your customer based on your company's messages and style. The aesthetics you showcase in all that you do will draw in your customer.

Don't get too carried away with your product variation unless you know it is scalable. Everyone's situation is different, so it would be glib for me to tell you what and how to make your products. All I ask is that you really think it through. Your product variation and your revenue streams are intrinsically tied together. If, for example, your sole mission is to ship a few pallets of product every three days, you might be better off with a very small variation of product in the start, and grow into more later. The choice is ultimately yours, but remember that your production must be scalable; scalable for physical growth, economic growth and emotional balance (not going crazy!).

Ultimately, there is a ceiling to your own physical (and mental) capabilities that you will eventually hit while growing your business as a solopreneur. If you want to put money in your pocket and grow your company into a large brand, you are going to need help. Whether it is hiring a graphic designer, a business coach, a copywriter or a soapmaker, you will need to delegate to further your success. While at first this endeavor may seem like a financial/cash flow setback, it will ultimately pay off. Hiring and delegating tasks is simply a sign of growth, and often, growth is associated with financial pain. Hence, growing pains.

If you do your accounting correctly and know your margins through and through, you might be surprised at how much is there to hire good help.

Create hype. Be bold, innovative and even weird if necessary. Develop a keen sense of how to attract people. This might be through intriguing questions in an email newsletter, or a zany billboard sign in a busy part of town. Whatever it is, make a plan. Develop an entire calendar year (before the year begins) on paper, showcasing each and every marketing tactic you can dream up. Fill the year with engaging ideas, promotions, deals, events, etc. with an aura that can *only* come from you and your company.

I would imagine after reading this book you might have more questions than answers. I say this not to shoot myself in the foot, but to suggest that if you really engaged yourself in some of the lessons, you might find yourself needing to find out more.

This, more than anything else, is why I wrote this book. I urge you to take control of your situation. These days, we have so much access to information! You can literally become an expert at anything with very little financial commitment, thanks to the world we now live in. If you don't know how to market, read a book. If you don't wish to ever make a sale, find a book on hiring sales representatives – they are out there. If you can't write, hire a copywriter to create your product descriptions.

You don't have any excuses. If you want to make your business work, you can. If you want to be successful, you can. For example, your geographic area doesn't limit your success, and thus your revenue. If you think it does, you aren't thinking big enough. You aren't' being bold in your thoughts, which will result in inaction.

You're gonna fail so hard.

You aren't going to get it right all the time. The bigger your company becomes, the bigger the risk in all the choices you make. That's just how it is in the world of owning your own business. It's okay to fail. I've wrecked literally thousands of pounds of product batches. I've wasted thousands and thousands of dollars on stupid purchases and investments. I've handled employees the wrong way by not being a strong enough leader. I've unknowingly insulted customers on social media. I've made an ass out of myself in front of really important people. There were years when we weren't profitable. There were *years* when I didn't know what the hell I was doing.

You will carry on some rendition of all these things as well. It's just part of it. Don't let it stop you from pursuing your end-all dream of running a successful soap and skin care company. Let each failure be a spur to your side, which is painful, but forces forward momentum.

But most of all, find out what you don't know. Learn. You can't learn from what you already know. Be ever-curious and act upon that curiosity. If you need your company to *be* a certain way, to *look* a certain way, to present itself in a certain way, but you don't know how to accomplish it, figure it out. Not knowing is no excuse. Ask people. Hire someone. Research. Do the gritty ground work required of you. Hustle.

Be an entrepreneur!

ABOUT THE AUTHOR

Benjamin Aaron is a business coach and consultant through The Lovin' Soap Studio. In addition to consulting and coaching, Benjamin engages in brand development through graphic design and copywriting for startups. Find out more at www.lovinsoap.com.

Together, Benjamin and Amanda also co-founded and direct a 501(c)3 not-for-profit organization, The Lovin' Soap Project, which aims to empower women in developing nations through the artisan trade of soap and skin care production. Find out more at www.lovinsoapproject.org.

Benjamin's purpose and passion in is to provide individuals with a new lease on life. So many of us live a life of quiet desperation. Mentally and emotionally, we handcuff ourselves every day and tell anyone who will listen why things just won't work out for us. Benjamin's aim is to put a stop to this and open lives up to the real, raw ambitions we all have. You must set goals if you want anything in life. He has mastered the true power of goal-setting, and he loves to show people how to set unique goals.

"A fulfilled life requires an emotional investment of your time, energy and resources. Decide what you want to pursue, no matter how big, and make large, recurrent investments into seeing its fulfillment."

~ Benjamin D. Aaron

www.lovinsoap.com
www.lovinsoapproject.com
bda7b9@gmail.com

NEED HELP?

We've discussed a lot in this book, and I know that it can be overwhelming to attempt new concepts, such as sales funneling through email marketing, or recurrently changing your website's information and banners, etc.

If you need my services, or the services of someone else, please feel free to contact me so I can help you move in the right direction.

~ Benjamin

SUGGESTED READING

- *The Power of Habit* by Charles Duhigg
- *Startupland* by Mikkel Svane
- *Marketing: A Love Story* by Bernadette Jiwa
- *Don't Make Me Think [Revisited]* by Steve Krug
- *PRE-SUASION: A Revolutionary Way to Influence and Persuade* by Robert Cialdini
- *Everybody Writes: Your Go-To Guide to Creating Ridiculously Good Content* by Ann Handley
- *Content Inc* by Joe Pulizzi
- *The New Rules of Marketing and PR* by David Meerman Scott
- *Pricing Handmade Soap for Profit* by Benjamin D. Aaron
- *How to Wholesale Your Handcrafted Soap* by Benjamin D. Aaron
- *The Success Principles* by Jack Canfield
- *The Hero and the Outlaw* by Margaret Mark
- *Hello, My Name is Awesome* by Alexandra Watkins
- *Contagious* by Jonah Berger
- *Launch* by Jeff Walker
- *Dot Com Secrets* by Russell Brunson
- *World-Class Warehousing and Material Handling* by Edward Frazelle
- *Inventory Accuracy: People, Processes, & Technology* by David J. Piasecki
- *Profit First* by Mike Michalowicz

Made in the USA
San Bernardino, CA
24 November 2017